Journal of Public Philosophy

THE LOGOS FOUNDATION

Issue 3

 Public Philosophy Press

First published by Public Philosophy Press 2022
Phoenix, AZ

Copyright © 2022 by Journal of Public Philosophy

All rights reserved. No part of this publication may be reproduced, stored or transmitted in any form or by any means, electronic, mechanical, photocopying, recording, scanning, or otherwise without written permission from the publisher. It is illegal to copy this book, post it to a website, or distribute it by any other means without permission.

General Editor, Kelly Fitzsimmons Burton

Cover art by Beth Ellen Nagle

Typesetting by Matthew Hicks

First edition

ISBN: 978-1-7365424-8-4

Contents

Preface i

Editor's Note iii

Contributors v

Articles

A Christmas 2021 Global Renaissance Manifesto
      Peter A. Redpath, Ph.D. 1

A Philosophical Call To Renew American Culture
      Peter A. Redpath, Ph.D. 43

The Homeschool Renaissance And The Battle Of The Arts
      Peter A. Redpath, Ph.D. 59

The Beautiful as a Dimension of Ethics Within the
      Platonic-Aristotelian Philosophy
      Kelly Fitzsimmons Burton, Ph.D. 75

Neo-Neo-Pythagoreanism: Number as Metaphysics,
      Mathematics as Human Life
      Jason Morgan, Ph.D. 105

Essays and Book Reviews

Exploring a Roadmap Toward Biblical Reconciliation
      Christopher Croom 141

Divine Law and The Social Contract
      Wyatt T. McIntyre 157

The Life of Abraham Lincoln
      Arturo Gastelum 167

Jonathan Edwards Among the Theologians
      Crisp, Oliver
      Arturo Gastelum 177

Preface

The *Journal of Public Philosophy* is sponsored by the Logos Foundation. The goal of the Journal is to publish papers, essays, and book reviews in the mode of classical philosophy. We seek to know the basic truths that are foundational for the common good, and a just and civil society.

The goal of public philosophy is to make the practice of philosophy more accessible and more relevant to students, scholars, and the broadly educated public. We hope to inspire all in the shared, rational pursuit of wisdom and in love of Being, Unity, the True, the Good, and the Beautiful.

Public philosophy is inspired by Socrates' engagement in dialogue in the agora, the shared public space of the city-state. It is the pursuit of the common good, our shared life together. We hope that others will join us in an ever broadening and deepening discussion.

The Logos Foundation serves academic education in Liberal Arts and Theology through The Logos Papers (thelogospapers.com), Logos Theological Seminary, Logos College of Liberal Arts, Logos Preparatory Academy, The Logos Curriculum, Logos Papers Press, and the Logos Study Center.

The *Journal of Public Philosophy* is published by Public Philosophy Press: www.publicphilosophypress.com

Kelly Fitzsimmons Burton, Ph. D.
General Editor

Editor's Note

The *Journal of Public Philosophy* was initially launched by students of Dr. Surrendra Gangadean, who made philosophy come alive for us and encouraged us to engage in public philosophy outreach.

Dr. Gangadean completed his work and went to glory on February 12, 2022. He was a giant in the faith and passed on a comprehensive vision for rebuilding the broken foundations in the church, the academy, and culture. His concern was to lay a deeper foundation in philosophy through what is clear to reason about God and man and good and evil; in theology through the Biblical narrative of creation, fall, and redemption, completed in the coming of Christ and articulated in the seven pillars of Christian theology; and lastly through the Historic Christian faith. His life's work was to clarify the philosophical foundation, theological foundation, and historical foundation with the goal of settling longstanding disputes in the church. He spent his life engaging the Modern and Post-modern challenges to the faith. He left a clear roadmap for the next Reformation.

We are grateful for the legacy that Dr. Gangadean left to us through the Logos Foundation, the over 100 Logos Papers he has written, his work as a College Professor, organizing pastor of Westminster Fellowship church, and his books: *Philosophical Foundation: A Critical Analysis of Basic Beliefs* (UPA, 2008; Forthcoming Public Philosophy Press 2022) and *Theological Foundation: A Critical Analysis of Christian Belief* (Forthcoming Logos Papers Press, 2022). He was a mentor to many of us, and we hope to advance his work to benefit future generations.

The *Journal of Public Philosophy* includes others that have a concern for public rationality and rebuilding the foundation for culture. If you are new to our publication, I invite you to explore the work of Dr. Gangadean, beginning with https://thelogospapers.com/.

Thank you for supporting Public Philosophy.

Yours,
Kelly Fitzsimmons Burton
General Editor
Journal of Public Philosophy

Contributors

Kelly Fitzsimmons Burton, Ph. D. is a professor of Philosophy and Religious Studies at Paradise Valley Community College in Phoenix, AZ. She is the author of *Retrieving Knowledge: A Socratic Response to Skepticism* (Public Philosophy Press, 2018) and *Reason and Proper Function: A Response to Alvin Plantinga* (Public Philosophy Press, 2019).

Christopher N. Croom, M.BEx. is a Ph.D. Student of Practical Theology with a focus in Moral Theology at Columbia International University Seminary. A husband and father of four, Christopher is also the founder of CROSS & Culture, LLC, an education and blog space dedicated to edifying Church leaders and servants of Christ on how to mingle faith and reason to strengthen the Church and engage the culture and influence the institutions of America toward righteousness.

Arturo Gastelum is a Ph. D. student in Humanities with an emphasis in Philosophy at Faulkner University. His research interest is in the relationship between faith and reason.

Wyatt-James "Wyatt" T. McIntyre holds a BS in Liberal Studies, and a BS in Marketing, as well as a Master of Arts in Ministry, Master of Arts in Biblical Apologetics, Master of Business Administration, Master of Divinity and a Master of Theology in Christian Apologetics. Aside from his current ministry work he is currently employed as the Director of Market Research for a Commercial Real Estate Company in the Chicagoland Metro Area.

Jason Morgan is Associate Professor at Reitaku University in Chiba, Japan.

Peter A. Redpath, Ph. D. is retired Full Professor of Philosophy at St. John's University, New York, and is CEO of the Aquinas School of Leadership, Rector of the Adler-Aquinas Institute and Senior Fellow at the Center for the Study of The Great Ideas. He is author of twelve philosophical books [including *The Moral Psychology of St. Thomas Aquinas: An Introduction to Ragamuffin Ethics* (En Route Books & Media, 2017), *A Not-So-Elementary Christian Metaphysics*, Vol. 2 (En Route Books & Media, 2016), and *A Not-So-Elementary Christian Metaphysics*, Vol. 1 (En Route Books & Media, 2nd printing, 2015) and numerous articles and book reviews.

A Christmas 2021 Global Renaissance Manifesto: A Collaborative Call for a World Cultural Renaissance through Establishment of a Global Commonsense Solidarity Union (GCSU)

Peter A. Redpath, Ph.D.

Introduction: Why a Need Presently Exists for a Global Cultural Renaissance and a Global Commonsense Solidarity Union (GCSU):

Whether liberal, conservative, or of some other political persuasion, well known to anyone with political common sense is that the contemporary world is increasingly becoming subjected to arbitrary totalitarian political mandates that fly in the face of the exercise of traditional Western and global civil liberties and natural human rights. Defenders of civil liberties and natural human rights do not: (1) tend to silence exercise of the free speech of those who disagree with them and banish it from the public square; (2) through *ad hominem* and *strawman arguments*, incline to demonize as *conspiracy* theorists those who intellectually oppose them; and (3) engage, or advocate engaging, in practices that violate the Nuremberg Code, and, in some instances, seek to overturn it as antiquated.

As long ago as the first half of the twentieth century, leading liberal thinkers *like the benevolent* pagan Mortimer J. Adler were warning Americans that *something was radically despotic about Modern and Enlightenment scientific positivism and the reductionistic principles related to truth that it accepted*, which were starting to predominate in the psychological disposition of the Western educated class from which our cultural and political leaders tend to arise.

For example, at a 1941 New York City "Conference on Science, Philosophy and Religion," *the self-declared politically liberal, globalist, and democratic socialist* Adler criticized the "founding members" and "eminent representatives of the various academic disciplines" from mostly American colleges and universities (but also attending members from learned societies, and academic disciplines that extended beyond philosophy, religion, and modern science to include social scientists of different sorts—such as, historians and humanistic scholars) for organizing and, or, participating in a meeting that, from the start, *in its principles*, was doomed to fail. To host a meeting of such a nature to accomplish some aim, purpose, which could not be "accomplished in the ordinary processes of our academic life—in classrooms, faculty meetings, or the sessions of learned societies," Adler had maintained that its organizers would have to be able rationally to "justify this Conference as trying to do something which is not, and perhaps cannot be, accomplished in the ordinary processes of our academic life—in classrooms, faculty meetings, or the sessions of learned societies." (For the full text of Adler's entire Conference address cited herein, see: http://www.ditext.com/adler/gp.html)

According to Adler, all the participants had assembled at this Conference because, for different reasons and in different degrees, they had all shared "an uneasiness about something" they had called their "present situation." They had come to this Conference because they were crying "with one voice that all's not right with the world." From some explanations he had heard given at the meeting about the chief aim, purpose, for their gathering—which had made mention of the World War II conflict "between democracy and totalitarianism in the political arena" or the then-current battle "between individualism and collectivism in the economic sphere"—Adler had asked the participants, "If that were the full nature of the crisis, why should we waste time talking about science, philosophy and religion?"

In answer to that rhetorical question, Adler gave the following reply:

> The fact that we have chosen to consider three major components of human culture should indicate that we all have a vague sense of cultural disorder as the root of our troubles, *as the source of a threatening doom* (our italics). Far from being prime movers, Hitler and Mussolini, or, if you wish, the Stalins and Chamberlains, are but paranoiac puppets, dancing for a moment on the crest of the wave—the wave that is the historic motion of modern culture to its own destruction. A culture is not killed by political conflicts, even when they attain the shattering violence of modern warfare; nor by economic revolutions, even when they involve the dislocations of modern mass uprisings.
>
> A culture dies of diseases which are themselves cultural. It may be born sick, as modern culture was, or it may decay through insufficient vitality to overcome the disruptive forces present in every culture; but, in any case, cultural disorder is a cause and not an effect of the political and economic disturbances which beset the world today.
>
> The health of a culture, like the health of the body, consists in the harmonious functioning of its parts. Science, philosophy and religion are certainly major parts of European culture; their distinction from one another as quite separate parts is certainly the most characteristic cultural achievement of

modern times. But if they have not been properly distinguished, they cannot be properly related; and unless they are properly related, properly ordered to one another, cultural disorder, such as that of modern times, inevitably results.

According to Adler, in actuality their Conference had been called to consider the psychological illness of American culture and to seek and effect remedies for that cultural disorder. One reason they had to call a special meeting to do this was because the nature of the contemporary university, with its separate academic *departments* of scientists, philosophers, and theologians, or teachers of religion, had "long failed to *communicate* with one another" (our italics).

"The structure of a modern, *Enlightenment* (our addition in italics) university, with its departmental separations," where academic members do not tend to communicate with each other, "and its total lack of order among specialized disciplines," he added,

> represents perfectly the disunity and chaos of modern culture. Since nothing can be expected of the professors *locked up in their departmental cells* (our italics), since reforming our institutions of higher learning (to make them truly universities) seems to be impossible, since the ordinary processes of academic life manifest the very defects which must be remedied, the professors have been assembled under the special auspices of this Conference with the hope that lines of communication can be established. That done, one might even hope for communication to lead to mutual understanding, and thence to agreement about the truths which could unify our culture.
>
> If what I have said is not the purpose of this Conference, I can see no justification for it whatsoever. The fact that all the professors gathered mention

the Present Crisis, without trying to agree about its nature and causes; the fact that they manifest some concern about Democracy, without trying to define it and understand its roots; the fact that, in a baffling variety of senses, they refer to Science, Philosophy and Religion, without trying to solve the intricate problem of the relationship of these disciplines,—all this amounts to nothing.

An undertaking of this sort is not needed to make professors think or talk this way. Nor is it needed to give them an opportunity to write and read papers which do credit to their specialized scholarly achievements. Unless this be a Conference in more than name only, unless it be a concerted effort to reach a common understanding of our cultural failure and a common program for its reform, this gathering will be as vacuous and futile as many another solemn conclave of professors, advertised by high-sounding and promising titles.

Adler then told the participants there present that, if he had accurately stated the only purpose that could rationally justify the existence of the Conference, "it cannot possibly succeed." *No matter how good it might be*, he added, *even the best of all possible conferences could not succeed in reforming modern culture. Nor could anyone even succeed correcting one of the main causes of its disorder—modern education with its narrow, reductionistic, underlying principles of scientific positivism.* And the chief reason for this was because "one cannot expect the professors to understand what is wrong with modern culture and modern education, for the simple reason that that would require them to understand what is wrong with their own mentality." Since professors come to a conference of this sort with the intention of speaking their minds but not of changing them, with a willingness to listen but not to learn, with the kind of tolerance which delights in a variety of opinions and abominates the unanimity of agreement," he added, "it is preposterous to suppose that this Conference can even begin to realize the only ends which justify the enterprise."

Instead of a conference related to science, philosophy, religion, and democracy, Adler had maintained, they needed:

> a conference about the professors of science, philosophy and religion, especially American professors whose intellectual attitudes express a false conception of democracy. The defects of modern culture are the defects of its intellectual leaders, its teachers and savants. The disorder of modern culture is a disorder in their minds, a disorder which manifests itself in the universities they have built, in the educational system they have devised, in the teaching they do, and which, through that teaching, perpetuates itself and spreads out in ever widening circles from generation to generation. It is a little naive, therefore, to suppose that the professors can be called upon to solve the problem of the relationship of science, philosophy and religion in our education and in our culture—as naive as it would be to invite the professors to participate in a conference about what is wrong with the professors.
>
> With a few notable exceptions, the members of this Conference represent the American academic mind. It is that fact itself which makes it unnecessary, as well as unwise, for me to make any effort in the way of reasoning. I know too well, from much experience, the opinions of this audience, and of all the professors they represent—about the nature and relationship of science, philosophy and religion.

According to Adler, (1) the prevailing opinions of American college and university professors in 1941 about the natures of science, philosophy, religion, and democracy were those of scientific positivism and *were wrong*; and (2) American culture at the time was suffering grave disorders precisely because it embodied these positivistic opinions as first principles of imagining, judging, reasoning, and understanding. As a result, while some rational point had existed at the time for someone to host such a conference with the aim of fixing the then-prevalent errors, asking college and university professors to do so was pointless, was like asking incendiaries to help extinguish a forest fire.

He went on to charge most of the Conference participants of being scientific positivists, of only paying lip-service to admitting that some truth exists in the disciplines of philosophy and religion. And while he said he knew that enough varieties of positivism exist to allow "the professors to retain their individuality," he insisted that *behind the many technical jargons lay a generic doctrine: the affirmation that the whole of truth lies in contemporary mathematical-physical science, and the denial that any truth resides in the disciplines of philosophy and religion.*

While, upon hearing his claim that some truth resides in philosophy and religion, he said professors at the meeting would smile, bemuse themselves at his simplicity, deny the truth of what he had said, and cordially ask, "Whoever heard anyone, except a few violent extremists, flatly denying philosophy and religion; as a matter of fact, such dogmatic denials are made only by a small circle of 'philosophers' who blatantly advertise themselves as positivists. The very presence at this Conference of scientists, philosophers and theologians shows that the representatives of the several disciplines respect each other; the fact that they are willing to listen to each other's papers shows the spirit of cooperation which prevails among them."

Some Conference members would even start "to wonder about the sanity (our italics) of those who talk about the disorder and disunity of modern culture. The real problem of this Conference must be the perils of Democracy; it certainly cannot be the issue about positivism."

Despite such attempts at politely disagreeing with him, Adler repeated his charge. *He said that then-contemporary American professors were, by and large, scientific positivists.* And he immediately added that "the most serious threat to Democracy is the positivism of the professors, which dominates every aspect of modern education and is the central corruption of modern culture. *Democracy has much more to fear from the mentality of its teachers than from the nihilism of Hitler* (our italics). It is the same nihilism in both cases, but Hitler's is more honest and consistent, less blurred by subtleties and queasy qualifications, and hence less dangerous.

Among other claims, Adler added:

> Religion cannot be regarded as just another aspect of culture, one among many human occupations, of indifferent importance along with science and art, history and philosophy. Religion is either the supreme human discipline, because it is God's discipline of man, and as such dominates our culture, or it has no place at all. The mere toleration of religion, which implies indifference to or denial of its claims, produces a secularized culture as much as militant atheism or Nazi nihilism.

He stated that the philosophers at the time who thought all the significant questions men ask are answerable by "scientific reason" or not at all were *philosophical naturalists* in the sense of philosophically defending the positivism of scientists (*mathematical physicists*, our addition) "who think that science alone is valid knowledge, and that science is enough for the conduct of life." If the philosophy professors were positivists, they had to be philosophical naturalists. Adler stated that such people "dishonor themselves as well as religion by tolerating it when, all equivocations overcome, they really think that faith is superstition, just as they really think philosophy is opinion. The kind of positivism and naturalism which is revealed in all their works and all their teaching is at the root of modern secularized culture."

In saying this, Adler added that his reason for so doing had a moral foundation. He had wished "the professors might examine their conscience in the light of clearly defined issues, and acknowledge plainly what they really think. I know, of course, that that is too much to hope for. But since actions speak louder than words, no one who understands the issues will be deceived by what the professors have to say, however much they fool themselves." In and of itself, the professorial conduct of the Conference belied "the professorial speech, the polite discourse, the insulting tolerance, which conceals the dismissal of philosophy as opinion and religion as superstition behind expressions of specious respect."

Even though the claim was made by an ethnic Jew, Mortimer Adler's assertion that modern positivistic college and university professors—*scientific naturalists*—were worse than Hitler and, *in their principles, were as bad as militant atheists and nihilists*, might shock the moral sensibilities of some readers of this Manifesto. Some might react to it with the same sort of moral indignation as those professors who had attended the 1941 Conference at which he had spoken. As a result, on the basis of their high moral and professional standards, they might decide that they could never support, or sign on, to a document such as this one.

Nonetheless, they might want to reconsider the wisdom and prudence of such a psychological reaction. Adler's assertions about Hitler and militant atheism, nihilism, scientific naturalism, and the disorders that consistent application of its principles necessarily produces within a culture is simply an analogous transposition of the philosophical claims brought by Socrates against the Ancient Greek sophists Gorgias Polus, Callicles, and Thrasymachos in Plato's dialogues *Gorgias* and *Republic*. Strictly speaking, *because the principles they repeatedly inculcated into the souls of their students were essentially totalitarian, these sophists were culturally worse and more damaging to Ancient Greek culture than were the despotic politicians, paranoid puppets—like Archelaeus— that they had produced.* Analogously considered, had the readers who today negatively react to what this Manifesto reports Adler had said in 1941 been alive in Athens in 399 B.C., intellectually and morally they would have sided with the sophists and against Socrates at his trial. Apart from being morally wrong, they would have been philosophically wrong and on the wrong side of history—just as they will be now!

In continuing his acerbic analysis and critique, Adler mentioned that the failure of the Conference to do the only work which had rationally justified its existence had perfectly symbolized:

> the absence of cultural community in the modern world; worse than that, it justifies the most extreme pessimism about an impending catastrophe, for until THE professors (that is, the scientific naturalists) and their culture are liquidated, the resolution of modern problems—a resolution which history demands shall be made—will not even begin. The tower of Babel we are building invites another flood (our italics, and our parenthetical addition).
>
> The failure of this Conference is due not only to the fact that the professors are, for the most part, positivists; but even more so to their avoidance of what is demanded for fruitful intellectual procedure. Unlike the mediaeval man of learning, the modern professor will not subject himself to the rigors of public disputation. He emasculates discussion by treating it as an exchange of opinions, in which no one gains or loses because everyone keeps his own. He is indocile in the sense that, beyond the field of science, he cannot be instructed, because he acknowledges no ignorance.
>
> Hence anyone who would try to instruct him about philosophical or religious truths would be regarded as authoritarian, as trying to impose a doctrine. He is scandalized by the very notion of a commonly shared truth for all men. Even though such truth can be attained only by the free activity of each

mind, the fact that no mind is free to reject the truth seems like an infringement upon his sacred liberties. What he means by truth in science and by agreement among scientists permits him to talk as if he were a truth-seeker and willing to agree; but that is because the contingent and tentative character of scientific knowledge so perfectly fits the egoism, the individualism, the libertinism, of the modern mind.

The greater necessity and finality of truth in philosophy and religion oblige a mind in ways it will not suffer. On fundamental questions, which means all the questions beyond the scope of science, he wishes to keep a thoroughly open mind forever; he wishes neither to be convinced of anything nor to convince anyone. Hence he would not participate in a conference which required everyone to agree upon the fundamental questions to be answered, and measured its success by the degree to which such answers were commonly achieved as a result of the most patient discussion.

After finishing indicating what he called "the significance of this Conference for the state of our culture, *and the doom it forebodes*" (our addition), Adler concluded his talk by stating he wanted briefly to indicate the relation his analysis had "to the crisis of Democracy." Holding as a conclusion that he maintained could "be demonstrated in terms of the truths of moral and political philosophy," he stated the positivists can say "nothing." According to them:

> Outside the sphere of science nothing can be demonstrated, and the proposition that Democracy is the best political order certainly lies outside the sphere of science. What is neither self-evident nor demonstrable must be an opinion, which attracts or repels us emotionally. Anyone who denies

that philosophy is knowledge denies, of course, the self-evidence of moral principles and the validity of moral demonstrations.

Hence the professors can be for Democracy only because they like it, not because they know it is right. They talk a great deal about natural rights and the dignity of man, but this is loose and irresponsible talk, in which they lightly indulge because they do not mind contradicting themselves. *There are no natural rights if there is no natural moral law, which is binding upon all men everywhere in the same way. Man has no dignity if he is not a rational animal, essentially distinct from the brutes by reason of the spiritual dimension of his being. This should be enough to make clear that positivists are forced to deny the rights and dignity of man, or hold such views only as prejudice, rationally no better than Hitler's prejudices to the contrary. But to reinforce the point that the professors have no grounds for any of their fine feelings, let me add that the same facts which warrant man's dignity as an end to be served by the state also imply that man has an immortal soul, and a destiny beyond the temporal order. In short, one cannot have reasons for affirming Democracy and at the same time deny the truths of philosophy and religion* (our italics).

Beyond intrinsic human dignity, Adler should have added that the existence of an immortal human soul is a necessary condition for the existence of 'scientific' truth. Such *scientific* truth (abstractly considered truth that in the here and now exists as a truth abstractly judged to be true always and everywhere), *such uncommon commonsense* truth, can only exist in the *intellectual soul* of a scientist in the present time as a truth generated as part of a providentially-guided order. It cannot exist in a brute animal. Nor can it exist in an angel or in God (because Angelic and Divine science are not human science, and brutes have no science at all).

Unhappily for Adler, in 1941 he had not had the advantage of reading C. S. Lewis's masterful monograph, *The Abolition of Man* (which was published two years later). Had Adler had the opportunity to have read this work, we have no doubt he would have agreed with Lewis's assessment that, without the existence of a judging and reasoning principle existing within an embodied, animal soul (a rational center of psychological influence essentially connected to the human body as a prudential command and control moral principle, cause, able rationally to regulate and constrain the human passions so as to enable an abstract, syllogistic intellect, with total emotional impartiality, to execute commands of commonsense, right reason, within the human emotions), "man is not man," and, strictly speaking, "Christian" man can never be "Christian" man.

As Lewis said, "The Chest-Magnanimity-Sentiment," animal rationality (what St. Thomas Aquinas considered to be a specific difference unique to a human animal, allowing an immortal, rational soul to overflow into a sentient part of the same soul, where Aquinas located "common sense," deliberative "choice," and the moral virtue of "prudence")—"these are the indispensable liaison officers between cerebral man and visceral man." St. Thomas and Lewis had maintained that, without embodiment of prudential moral principles within the human soul (moral principles that enable, cause, human beings to be abstractly impartial judges and emotionally self-controlled decision-makers), what is thought to be, and is called, a "human soul" is actually a disembodied spirit, or disembodied intellect.

Such a disembodied entity does not correspond to the Christian understanding of a human soul. And a soulless body (a body in which spirit is not an animating principle of life, growth, and development of a living, sentient, organic matter) does not correspond to a Christian understanding of a human body. Lewis adds, "It may even be said that it is by this middle element (the rationally-sentient soul) that man is man: for by his intellect he is mere spirit and by his appetite mere animal." (C. S. Lewis, *The Abolition of Man: Reflections on Education with Special Reference to the Teaching of English in the Upper Forms of School* (New York: Macmillan, 1955), 34; St. Thomas Aquinas, *Summa theologiae*, I, q. 77, a. 3, *respondeo*)

It is within reason existing as such a free, command and-control principle of the sense faculties and emotions in the animal part of the human soul that St. Thomas most precisely locates deliberative choice, common sense, the moral virtue of prudence, and our specific, human difference! The resulting composite is an animal that senses with its intellect and intellectualizes with its senses: an animal able personally to execute animal activity in its highest form, in a *humanly soulful way*: simultaneously abstractly (calmly), syllogistically, and commonsensically, deliberatively, passionately, concretely with prudence, in touch with sense reality in the individual situation—a truly scientific animal!

By generating the faculty of sensory reasoning, sentient, command-and-control reason (a faculty St. Thomas calls "particular reason"—which he claims corresponds to "instinct" in brute animals (S. th., I, q. 78, a. 4, *respondeo*; I, q. 78, a. 4, ad 5) —Aquinas maintains that the intellectual soul generates a personally-human, *animal rationality* (one that reasons abstractly and syllogistically when not focusing attention on concrete, individual, animal activity) to overflow through the sensitive part of the soul into the human body and sense reality as a personally-animal, command and-control, prudential ruling principle of the sensitive faculties, passions, and all their activities. In so doing, the rational part of the soul enables the sensitive part to achieve its animal perfection as an acting, sensitive soul, an acting person (as St. John Paul II was fond of saying)—something that no other animal soul can achieve: being a deliberative (free), commonsensical animal!

As Lewis prudently observes, "Without the aid of trained emotions, the intellect is powerless against the animal organism." To this sage observation, Lewis adds: "In battle it is not syllogisms that will keep the reluctant nerves and muscles to their post in the third hour of bombardment. The crudest sentimentalism . . . about a flag, or a country, or a regiment will be of more use. We were told it all long ago by Plato. As the king governs by his executive, so Reason in man must rule the mere appetites by means of the spirited element. The head rules the belly through the chest." Absent such training, Lewis maintains, "We make men without chests (what, today, we commonly call 'snowflakes,' those who are 'Woke') and expect of them virtue and enterprise. We laugh at honour and are shocked to find traitors in our midst. We castrate and bid the geldings to be fruitful." As Lewis warns us, the practical result of an education that denies such a reason and such a reality must be "the destruction of the society which accepts it." (Lewis, *The Abolition of Man*, 33–35)

Such a society is the one Adler describes in concluding his scathing critique of "the sort of democracy to which the professors are sentimentally attached." He states that such a democracy can never exist in reality. Its existence

> cannot be demonstrably proved, for theirs is an essentially false conception. The social order they would like to preserve is the anarchic individualism, the corrupt liberalism, which is the most vicious caricature of Democracy. Objecting to any inequalities in value, objecting to any infringement of absolute individual liberty by loyalties and obligations to superior goods, they want a democracy without hierarchy and without authority. In short, they want chaos, not order, a society in which everyone will be as free as if he lived alone, a community in which common bonds will not bind the individual at all. Even when they speak enthusiastically about this false ideal, the professors seldom claim that they have rational grounds for its defense. The very fact that they so frequently refer to democracy, not as a government or as a political order, but as a way of life, reveals them as exponents of a false religion. This religion of democracy is no

better than the religion of fascism. One is the idolatry of individual liberty as the other is the worship of collective might.

One of the greatest achievements of the modern world is the discovery of the moral and political reasons for the democratic ideal, as well as actual experimentation in the field of democratic processes. But though it be in this sense a child of modern times, Democracy will not be fully achieved until modern culture is radically reformed. Science contributes nothing whatsoever to the understanding of Democracy. Without the truths of philosophy and religion, Democracy has no rational foundation. In America at present it is at best a cult, a local prejudice, a traditional persuasion. Today it is challenged by other cults which seem to have more might, and no less right, so far as American ability to defend democracy rationally is concerned.

For all these reasons I say we have more to fear from our professors than from Hitler. It is they who have made American education what it is, both in content and method: in content, an indoctrination of positivism and naturalism; in method, an exhibition of anarchic individualism masquerading as the democratic manner. Whether Hitler wins or not, the culture which is formed by such education cannot support what democracy we have against interior decay.

If I dared to raise my voice as did the prophets in ancient Israel, I would ask whether the tyrants of today are not like the Babylonian and Assyrian kings— instruments of Divine justice, chastening a people who had departed from the way of truth. In the inscrutable Providence of God, and according to the nature of man, a civilization may sometimes reach a rottenness which only fire can expunge and cleanse. If the Babylonians and Assyrians were destroyers, they were also deliverers. Through them, the prophets realized, God purified His people. Seeing the hopelessness of working peaceful reforms among a people who had shut their eyes and hardened their hearts, the prophets almost prayed for such deliverance, through the darkness of destruction, to the light of a better day. So, perhaps, the Hitlers in the world today are preparing the agony through which our culture shall be reborn. Certainly if it is part of the Divine plan to bless man's temporal civilization with the goodness of Democracy, that civilization must be rectified. It is probably not from Hitler, but from the professors, that we shall ultimately be saved.

As Adler clearly shows, contemporary Enlightenment colleges and universities are essentially designed to drive out common sense and moral prudence from the psyche of students and convince them that the only species of understanding (common sense) in which truth exists is mathematical physics. In doing this, they cause students to become anarchists, unteachable, 'Woke' individuals out of touch with reality who, like their Enlightened professors, cannot tolerate to listen or to speak to or with anyone who disagrees with them.

Common sense is simply some understanding of first principles that cause some organizational whole to have the unity it has that causes it to tend to behave the way it does. Most of the time, most of us have little of it. When we do, this is because we possess an understanding common to anyone who intellectually grasps the nature of some organization, the way the parts (causal principles) of a whole incline to organize to generate organizational existence, unity, and action. Strictly speaking, common sense is the habit of rightly (commonsensically) applying first principles of understanding as measures of truth in immediate and mediated judgment, choice, and reasoning! Considered as such, it is the first measure of right (or commonsense) understanding and reasoning. Strictly speaking, only a morally and intellectually prudential person can develop this psychological disposition. It is a necessary condition for anyone to possess to become a real scientist—an emotionally impartial judge of truth and psychologically stable human being.

Before being taught outside the home, children generally learn some common sense by first becoming teachable at home—developing the moral virtue of *docilitas* (docility) from parents and from their individual *conscience (which, according to Aquinas, is the habit of prudence acting as judge, jury, witness, and prosecution of personal choices: Note—a person with no moral prudence is incapable of having a conscience)*. Unless human beings become habitually inclined to regulate our human emotions by the moral virtue of prudence, which is simply a species of common sense, human beings tend to become psychologically disordered, anarchists, barbarians. Worse than this, as the 1960s political radical Thomas Merton has well documented in his masterpiece "A Devout Meditation in Memory of Adolf Eichmann," in his monograph *Raids on the Unspeakable* (New York, New Directions Publishing Corporation, 1964), we tend to become psychologically unhealthy, morally depraved, insane *little Eichmanns*.

Reporting about one of the most disturbing facts he had discovered in the 1961 Eichmann trial in Jerusalem was that a psychiatrist who had examined him had pronounced Eichmann *perfectly sane*. Merton said he did not doubt this at all, and that is precisely why he found it disturbing. Had all the Nazis had been psychotics, Eichmann's appalling cruelty would have made him easier for Merton to understand. Much more difficult for him to comprehend was "this calm, 'well balanced,' unperturbed official conscientiously going about his desk work, his administrative job which happened to be the supervision of mass murder." (p. 45)

According to the psychological profile given of him by the psychiatrist, Eichmann "was thoughtful, orderly, unimaginative. He had a profound respect for system, for law and order. He was obedient, loyal, faithful officer of a great state. He served his government very well." (p. 45) He was simply a middle-management, Enlightenment-educated bureaucrat *with a dysfynctional conscience* doing his Enlightenment job.

Merton found Eichmann's "sanity" disturbing because (like Adler, Lewis, and all psychologically healthy human beings), he equated "sanity with a sense of justice, with humanness, with prudence, with the capacity to love and understand other people. We rely on the sane people of the world to preserve it from barbarism, madness, destruction. And now it begins to dawn on us that it is precisely the same sane ones who are the most dangerous." (p. 46)

Like Adler and Lewis, Merton started to reflect upon the meaning being *psychologically healthy, sane* in an Enlightenment world in which the meaning of a concept of sanity reduces human rationality to that of an intellect separated from an animal body, or restricted to brute animal nature. In both cases, like Adler and Lewis, he recognized that, by removing from a person the ability to have an animal rationality to control animal emotions, a human being necessarily becomes psychopathic, a robotic artificial intelligence or a wild animal that excludes love, moral prudence, and a healthy conscience from human life, considers love "irrelevant, and destroys our capacity to love other human beings, to respond to their needs and their sufferings, to recognize them as persons, to apprehend their pain as one's own. . . . Evidently this is not necessary for 'sanity' at all. It is a religious notion, a spiritual notion, a Christian notion." (p. 47)

In calling sanity "a Christian notion" Merton did not mean to imply that only Christians can be, or are, morally prudent, sane, or have a healthy conscience. He knew that history belied such a claim. Like Adler, Lewis, and Aquinas, he meant that being psychologically healthy, sane, morally prudent, essentially involves recognizing, like real Christians do, that a human being has an immortal soul possessed of a personal dignity and inalienable human rights that exists within a providentially guided order governed by a just and loving God. Even Christians, he said, can and do "cling to a certain set of Christian formulas, and fit them into a Totalist Ideology. Let them talk about justice, charity, love, and the rest. These words have not stopped some sane men from acting very soundly and cleverly in the past." (p. 48)

Those who recognize we live in such a providentially ordered world, we *add*, necessarily recognize that we live in some organizational whole in which our present way of existing is essentially connected to our future—that, in some way, we are incompletely *what we are to become, are essentially related to something that does not yet exist: our selves* as we are coming to human completion. Unless we accept the reality of a providential order in which some intellectual being (like a Creator God) exists capable, in the present, of intellectually straddling the present and the future and, *somehow making intelligible to us, how we can be essentially related to something that does not yet exist, and actually causing this relationship to be, we ask*, "How is this really possible? If this relationship is not real, does not exist, *is not* our real situation, the world we inhabit, essentially anarchic, insane?

Within such a world, how can we ever possess common sense or the virtue of moral prudence, a health conscience, or any conscience at all?" Moreover, how can a natural moral law binding upon all human beings everywhere in the same way—and the natural human rights and human dignity that essentially flow from it—exist if the virtue of prudence does not exist? As Adler said, "Man has no dignity if he is not a rational animal, essentially distinct from the brutes by reason of the spiritual dimension of his being."

And what is to become of sanity as a sign of psychological health, as a human virtue? Sanity is only a virtue if it is a psychological disposition existing in the human imagination, and in the conceiving, judging, and reasoning faculties of a human soul regulated by intellectual and moral prudence. Precisely because Eichmann's moral imagination was unmoored from, out of touch with, reality and lacked ordinary, human common sense, it was dull, insane. And so, too, were his conceiving, judging, and reasoning faculties.

As a result, he was totally, or almost, completely devoid of a conscience, completely insane.

In the Enlightenment world of Adolf Eichmann and those who think about being sane the way he did (as scientific positivists fighting each other "for power over the whole world"), in an article entitled "Letter to an Innocent Bystander" (in *Raids on the Unspeakable*), Merton asks whether any of "us" who oppose "them," including those who passively resist "them"—quietly biding our time to act—are really engaged in the "form of action"? While waiting for a time to strike might not be inertia, according to Merton, this "is only true, when one is resisting, and knows why, and to what end, he is resisting, and whom he must resist. Unless our waiting implies knowledge and action we will find ourselves waiting for our own distraction and nothing more. A witness of a crime, who just stands by and makes a mental note of the fact that he is an innocent bystander, tends by that very fact to become an accomplice." (55)

Merton asserts that "our" confusion in the face of contemporary global political power struggles by global elites "enables 'them' to use us, and to pit us against one another, for their own purposes. Our guilt, our deep resentment, do nothing to preserve us from a shame for fate. On the contrary, our resentment is what fits us most perfectly to be 'their' instruments." Our inability to know how to react to them, our seemingly helpless inertia, prevents us from being able to claim we are innocent. "It is the source of our guilt." (55-56)

By "our guilt" Merton does not mean all of "us" who presently oppose them. He tells us, "We are the intellectuals who have taken for granted that we could be 'bystanders' and that our quality as detached observers could preserve our innocence and relieve us of responsibility." (54) He means intellectuals like himself—talented writers and speakers, philosophers, theologians, poets: liberal artists of different sorts who know how to recognize, and use their talent to fight, propaganda. Regarding such people, he asks:

Is non-participation possible? Can complicity be avoided? You in your country and I in mine—you in your circle and I in my monastery: does the fact that we hate and resent tyranny and try to dissociate ourselves from it suffice to keep us innocent?

First, let us assume that we are clear who 'they' are. When I speak of 'them,' you will understand that I mean those special ones who seek power over 'all the others,' and who use us as instruments to gain power over the others. Just are three groups I am thinking of: 'they,' 'we,' and 'the others.' We, the intellectuals, stand in the middle and we must not forget that in the end everything depends on us.

It is therefore supremely important for us not to yield to despair, abandon ourselves to the 'inevitable' and identify ourselves with 'them.' Our duty is to refuse to believe that their way is 'inevitable.' And it is equally important for us not to set ourselves exclusively apart from 'the others' who depend on us and upon whom we ourselves also depend. (56)

"When we 'stand by' we try to think of ourselves as independent, as standing on our own feet. It is true that as intellectuals we ought to stand on our own feet— but one cannot learn to do this until he has first recognized the extent to which he requires the support of others. And it is our business to support one another against 'them,' not to be supported by 'them' and used to crush 'the others.' (58–59)

'They,' of course, have never really been in any position to support anyone. 'They' need us, but not our strength. They do not want us strong, but weak. It is our emptiness 'they' need, as justification for their own emptiness. That is why their support comes always, and only, in the form of bribes. We are nourished in order that we may continue to sleep. We are paid to keep calm, or to say things that do not disturb the unruffled surface of that emptiness from which, in due time, the spark and the blast must leap out and release, in all men, the grand explosion." (59)

As for the powerful ones, it is our job to recognize them even without their police, even before the establishment of their machinery. We must identify them wherever 'they' may appear, even though they may rise up in the midst of ourselves or among 'the others.' We must be able to recognize 'them' by what they are and not rest satisfied with what is said about them, by others or by themselves or above all by one of us! It is already rare for an intellectual to retain his sense of judgment when 'they' change their masks and re-shuffle their labels and put on different badges. Yet 'they' are always 'they.' It is to their obvious interest to bribe us to give them a new name, false identity, especially since, and doing so, we convince ourselves that we have made a brilliant discovery.

We must not let our vanity provide 'them' with false passports. (56–57)

As Étienne Gilson tells us in his celebrated *The Unity of Philosophical Experience* (New York: Charles Scribner's Sons, 1965), since, strictly speaking, Western culture (by which, broadly considered, Gilson essentially means the ancient Greek culture the ancient Romans had inherited, which was subsequently transfused by the ancient Church Fathers with Christian religious teachings, progressively increased by numerous artists, writers, philosophers, and scientists from the start of the Middle Ages to the present day) only exists in and through those who have created, and continue to create, it in the cultural institutions they have caused and continue to cause, *the West cannot be dying without such individuals being aware of it.* (271–272)

Regarding this inherited cultural enterprise, Gilson asks a very sobering question: "Can a social order, begotten by a common faith in the value of certain principles, keep on living when all faith in these principles is lost?" (272–273)

Best to illustrate the meaning of this question Gilson gives a summary description of two *principles* that, for him, constitute what, for brevity's sake, he calls "The Western Creed": two civilizational principles essential to the subsequent development of Western culture and all its cultural institutions.

Principle 1 is a firm belief of the ancient Greeks in the eminent dignity of human beings. As Gilson says:

> The Greeks of classical times never wavered in their conviction, that of all the things that can be found in nature, man is by far the highest, and that of all the things important for man to know, by far the most important is man. When Socrates, after unsuccessful attempts to deal with physical problems, made up his mind to dedicate himself to the exclusive study of man, he was making a momentous decision. 'Know thyself' is not only the key to Greek culture, but to the classical culture of the Western world as well. What the Greeks left to their successors was a vast body of knowledge related to man's nature and his various needs: logic, which is the science of how to think; several different philosophies, all of them culminating in ethics and politics, which are the sciences of how to live; remarkable specimens of history and political eloquence, related to the life of the city. As to what today we call positive science, the greatest achievements of the Greek genius were along the lines of mathematics, a knowledge which man draws from his own

mind without submitting to the degrading tyranny of material facts; and medicine, whose proper object is to ensure the well-being of the human body. And they stopped there, checked by an obscure feeling that the rest was not worth having, at least bit at the price which the human mind would have to pay for it: its freedom from matter, its internal liberty. (272–273)

Principle 2 is one that Gilson was convinced had culturally saved the ancient Greeks from constructing the monstrous idol which we, in the modern and contemporary West, have made with our own hands to modern and Enlightenment man's image and likeness. Hence, like Adler, Lewis, and Merton, Gilson identifies the second essential principle of Western culture and the Western Creed that we had inherited from the ancient Greeks to be "the conviction that reason is the specific difference of human beings." (p. 274)

Try to transform man's specific difference from human reason and turn it into universal consciousness existing separated from the individual human body like that of a logical android or that of brute animal with no reasoning faculty and Gilson maintains that we can no longer explain how a disembodied mind or a brute animal can regulate the human appetites and explain how human beings are moral agents:

> Man is best described as a rational animal; deprive man of reason and what is left of man is not man, but animal. This looks like a very commonplace statement, yet Western culture is dying wherever it is forgotten: for the rational nature of man is the only foundation for a rational system of ethics. Morality is essentially normality; for a rational being to act either without reason or contrary to its dictates is to act and behave not exactly as a beast, but as a beastly man, which is worse. For it is proper that a beast should act as a beast, that is, accord-

ing to its own nature; but it is totally unfitting for a man to act as a beast, because that means the total oblivion of his own nature, and hence his final destruction. (274)

Remarkable to Gilson is the centuries-long continuity by the subsequent generations within Western culture of these two principles inherited from the ancient Greeks. They had survived transmission to Christian culture, the Christian Middle Ages, renaissance humanism, the sixteenth-century Protestant Reformation, and even early modern discoveries in mathematical physics. So long as science remained faithful to its own philosophical, and chiefly metaphysical and moral, nature, Gilson says, "it remained the healthy exercise of reason, reason seeking to know because knowing is its natural function." (275–276)

He adds that,

> Even the most stupendous progress made by the physical and biological sciences entailed no disruption in the continuity of Western culture. While man remained in control of nature (*that is, retained the self-understanding of being a rational, and chiefly metaphysical and moral animal*), Western culture could survive. It was lost from the very moment nature began to control man (*that is, from the moment science became transformed into the Nietzschean will to power*). (276, italics is our addition)

Historically (in his little known, but prophetic, monograph, *The Terrors of the Year 2000*, written in 1948, and published by St. Michael's College of the University of Toronto, Canada, 1949), Gilson identified the precise date of this radical transformation to be the dropping of the Atomic Bomb on Hiroshima, Japan.

Within a few short pages, Gilson makes clear to his readers the nature of the terror he had envisioned besetting the Year Two Thousand. At the close of World War II, we human beings made our most astounding discovery, whose symbolism is more striking because it is involuntary: "the great secret that science has just wrested from matter is the secret of its destruction. To know today is synonymous with to destroy." (5–7)

Gilson maintains that the discovery of nuclear fission went far beyond being an inseparable union of good and evil involving: (1) "the most intimate revelation of the nature of the physical world," (2) "the freeing of the most powerful energy that has ever been held," and (3) "the most frightful agent of destruction which man has ever had at his disposal." He predicts, "The age of atomic physics will see the birth of a new world, as different from our own age as ours is from the world before steam and electricity." He says this new world presented human beings with a tragic dilemma. We know so many things today that our science might preclude our ability to control our own domination. In former times, Gilson states, we human beings mastered nature by obeying her. From now on, he claimed, we would master nature by destroying her. (7–9)

For once, to Gilson, the most daring prophecies of H. G. Wells appeared tame—because "in *The Island of Dr. Moreau* they were still only working to transform wild brutes into men; in the future society, it is men whom they will be transforming into brutes—to use them to foster the ends of a humanity thenceforth unworthy of the name." (9–11)

Gilson sees the dropping of the Atomic Bomb as a sign of the real possibility of the coming of the *Apocalypse*, which he thinks had been announced by Friedrich Nietzsche's Enlightenment declaration of the *Death of God*. Did any man more deserve the title of Antichrist than he who brought Zarathustra's terrifying message to the modern world? Gilson thinks not. He claims that Nietzsche's declaration of God's death marked in earnest the trans-valuation of values in the West and globally. Enlightenment man, Postmodern-man falsely-so-called, had explicitly started to put into action a plan formally to usurp God's place, become God. (11–14)

Gilson calls Nietzsche's declaration "the capital discovery of modern times." Compared to Nietzsche's discovery, he maintains that, no matter how far back we trace human history, we "will find no upheaval to compare with this in the extent or in the depth of its cause." Clearly, Gilson considers Nietzsche's declaration of God's death to a metaphysical revolution of the highest, widest, and deepest order. Nietzsche was metaphysical dynamite. He knew it, readily admitted it. "This is not just our imagination," Gilson asserts. All we have to do is read Nietzsche's *Ecce Homo* to find proof that what Gilson says is true: "I know my fate. A day will come when the remembrance of a fearful event will be fixed to my name, the remembrance of a unique crisis in the history of the earth, of the most profound clash of consciences, of a decree enacted against all that had been believed, enacted and sanctified right down to our days. I am not a man. I am dynamite." (14–16; while Gilson gives no specific reference to the location of this passage and the ones that follow it in Nietzsche's "*Ecce Homo*, see Friedrich Nietzsche, *The Philosophy of Nietzsche*, no editor or translator listed [New York: Random House, Modern Library, 1954], 858, 875. This one starts the section "Why I am a Fatality." See *Ecce Homo*, 923–933)

Clearly, to Gilson, the terrors of the year 2000 are, in root cause, metaphysical and moral. The chief clash of civilizations we face today is not between the politics of West and East, or the West and other political orders. It is a metaphysical and moral clash between the ancient and modern West.

Gilson said that, from time immemorial, we in the West have based our cultural creed and scientific inspiration upon the conviction that gods, or a God, existed. All of our Western intellectual and cultural institutions have presupposed the existence of a God or gods. No longer. All of a sudden, God no longer exists. Worse: He never existed! The implication is clear: "We shall have to change completely our every thought, word and deed. The entire human order totters on its base." (16–17)

If our entire cultural history depended upon the unswerving conviction that God exists, "the totality of the future must needs depend on the contrary certitude, that God does not exist." The metaphysical and terror now become evident in their depths. Nietzsche's message is a metaphysical and moral bomb more powerful than the atomic weapon dropped on Hiroshima: "Everything that was true from the beginning of the human race will suddenly become false." (17) Moreover, mankind alone must create for itself a new self-definition, which will become human destiny, the human project.

What is that destiny, project? *To destroy*. Gilson tells us Nietzsche knew that as long as we believe that what is dead is alive we can never use our creative liberty. Nietzsche knew and readily admitted his mission was to destroy. Hence, he said:

> When truth opens war on the age-old falsehood, we shall witness upheavals unheard of in the history of the world, earthquakes will twist the earth, the mountains and the valleys will be displaced, and everything hitherto imaginable will be surpassed. Politics will then be completely absorbed by the war of ideas and all the combinations of powers of the old society will be shattered since they are all built on falsehood: there will be wars such as the earth will never have seen before. It is only with me that great politics begin on the globe. . .. I know the intoxicating pleasure of destroying to a degree proportionate to my power of destruction.(16–17)

If Nietzsche spoke the truth about his project, which Gilson thinks he did, Gilson maintains that he was announcing the dawn of a new age in which the aim of postmodern Enlightenment culture, its metaphysical project, was to make war upon, to overthrow, traditional Western truths and values. To build our brave new world order, we have to overthrow the metaphysical and moral foundations of Western culture. "Before stating what will be true, we will have to say that everything by which man has thus far lived, everything by which he still lives, is deception and trickery." As Nietzsche said, "He who would be a creator, both in good and evil, must first of all know how to destroy and to wreck values." (16–17)

In fact, Gilson claims, our traditional Western values are being wrecked all around us, everywhere, under our feet. He says he had stopped counting "the unheard of theories thrown at us under names as various as their methods of thought, each the harbinger of a new truth which promises to create shortly, joyously busy preparing the brave new world of tomorrow by first of all annihilating the world of today." (17–18)

What, then, are we who oppose Nietzsche's project to do in the face of such a cataclysm? Nietzsche's plan, his mission and that of his progeny, is to destroy "today to create tomorrow." Gilson considers forgivable that we should not have anticipated Nietzsche's advent. "But," he says, "that we should not understand what he is doing while he is doing it right under our eyes, just as we were told he would do it—that bears witness to a stranger blindness. Can it really be that the herd of human being that is led to the slaughter has eyes and yet does not see?" Gilson's explanation for such a depth of blindness was that announcement of a catastrophe of such an order usually leaves us "but a single escape: to disbelieve it and, in order not to believe, to refuse to understand." (17–18)

Those who reject the escape of sticking our heads in the sand while we are sheepishly led to the slaughterhouse have another choice—to recognize the reality of the enemy we face and the nature of his project and reasonably to oppose it. Postmodern man (actually modern man on steroids) is essentially Nietzschean. And his "mad ambition" is impossible to achieve. We choose the way we can, not the way we wish. We might wish to become absolutely free creators, creators *ex nihilo*; but, at best, our wish is an impossible dream. To create in his turn *ex nihilo*, "man must first of all reestablish everywhere the void." (18–20)

This, then, has become *postmodern* Enlightenment man's project: mad ambition, everywhere to reestablish the void. On all sides, *postmodern* Enlightenment man feels Nietzsche's intoxicating joy, his mad delight, in the power of destruction. When Gilson says that Nietzsche is the Antichrist, he is speaking of Nietzsche metaphorically, much like Socrates says the Delphic oracle singled him out as an exemplar of wisdom in her cryptic message to his friend Chairephon that "no one is wiser Socrates." (Plato, Apology, 23B)

The Antichrist is *postmodern* Enlightenment man drunk "with the supremely lucid madness of a creature who would annihilate the obstacle which *being* places in the way of his creative ambitions. Such is the profound sense of our solemn and tragic adventure. Antichrist is not among us, he is in us. It is man himself, usurping unlimited creative power and proceeding to the certain annihilation of that which is, in order to clear the way for the problematic creation of all that will be." (*Terrors of the Year 2000*, 20–21)

While Gilson did not say so specifically, the Antichrist as Gilson had described him as embodied in Nietzsche is the secularized ghost of Renaissance humanism haunting the Earth, the postmodern attempt to *supplant creation with metaphysical epic poetry effected through the unbridled free spirit of artistic destruction*. No wonder, then, that Gilson would turn to a critic of Stéphane Mallermé's poetic project to find just the right phraseology to describe "precisely the sacrilegious effort whose meaning" he sought to unravel: "to construct a poetry which would have the value of preternatural creation and which would be able to enter into rivalry with the world of created things to the point of supplanting it totally." (21–22)

Postmodern man's Enlightenment project is universal surrealism, total release of human reason, of creative free spirit, from all metaphysical, moral, and aesthetic controls; the poetic spirit, the spirit of the artist gone totally mad with the intoxicating, surrealistic power of destruction. Once we destroy everything, nothing can stop us! Since the beginning of recorded time, God has gotten in the way of the artistic human spirit, has been the "eternal obstructor" to us being total self-creators. Now the tables are turned. With the advent of the *false postmodernity* announced by Nietzsche, we have entered "the decisive moment of a cosmic drama." (20) Protagoras and Musaios have become Dionysus.

"Everything is possible," Gilson tells us, "provided only that this creative spark which surrealism seeks to disclose deep in our being be preceded by a devastating flame." Since "the massacre of values is necessary to create values that are really new," André Breton's description of "the most simple surrealist act" becomes perfectly intelligible and throws dramatic light upon the increasingly cavalier destruction of innocent life by terroristic acts of mass murder in our own day: "The most simple surrealist act consists in this: to go down into the streets, pistol in hand, and shoot at random for all you are worth, into the crowd." (21–22) *If we truly want to decrease incidences of contemporary mass murder and other acts of terrorism and totalitarianism from the contemporary West and the world, no one gives a better understanding of the nature of these phenomena and analysis of how to eradicate them than does Gilson!*

Since we human beings tend to be slow learners, Gilson notes that we have needed some time to grasp the full implications of the postmodern project. We have gotten out of the habit of talking about things like "divine law," but we still hold onto its vestige in our enlightened, secularized appeals to "the voice of conscience." (23–25) Such appeals help us to pretend not to understand the catastrophic consequences of the grandiose sophistry of the postmodern project. If we pretend long enough that it does not exist, perhaps it will go away.

Unhappily, it will not. Gilson tells us that the father of *postmodern* man's existential project is Sisyphus, not Prometheus. Our destiny has become "the absurd" and "truly exhausting task" of perpetual self-invention without model, purpose, or rule. Having turned ourselves into gods, we do not know what to do with our divinity.

But what will happen to us when more of us start to realize that the voice of conscience is the reflection of nothing, a convenient illusion we have created to maintain the intoxicating joy of our own poetic and sophistic project? Even drunkards, at times, tire of their alcoholism.

Gilson admonishes us that our *postmodern* story is really quite old. He recounts the story of Samuel from the *Book of Samuel* (8:7–22) in which the Jewish people, tired of being free, asked the aging prophet Samuel to make them a king to judge them, like all other nations had. While Samuel was saddened by their request and saw it as a rejection of him as a judge, God told him to grant the people's wish with the forewarning of the sorts of bondage that would beset them once their wish was fulfilled. (26–27)

Having freed ourselves from divine rule, the necessary political consequence for postmodern man is political enslavement by a totalitarian State. Having refused to serve God, we have no one left to judge the State, no arbiter between us and the State. Hence, Gilson tells us:

> In every land and in all countries, the people wait with fear and trembling for the powerful of this world to decide their lot for them. They hesitate, uncertain among the various forms of slavery which are being prepared for them. Listening with bated breath to the sounds of those countries which fall one after the other with a crash followed by a long silence, they wonder in anguish how long will last this little liberty they still possess. The waiting is so tense that many feel a vague consent to slavery secretly germinating within themselves. With growing impatience, they await the arrival of the master who will impose on them all forms of slavery starting with the most degrading of all—that of mind. (28)

Finding ourselves totally free to engage in the perpetual task of endless self-creation, Gilson reports, we resemble a soldier on a twenty-four hour leave with nothing to do: totally bored in the tragic loneliness of an idle freedom we cannot productively use. (24) To Gilson's ears, the explosion of Hiroshima resounded a solemn metaphysical assertion of postmodern (better had he said "postmodern falsely-so-called") man's statement that, while we no longer want to be God's image, we can still be God's caricature. While we cannot create anything, we now possess the intoxicating power to destroy everything. As a result, feeling totally empty and alone, *postmodern* man (actually "modern Enlightenment man on steroids") offers, to anyone willing to take it, the futile freedom he does not know how to use. "He is ready for all the dictators, leaders of these human herds who follow them as guides and who are all finally conducted by them to the same place—the abbatoir" (the slaughterhouse). (28–29)

So, then, now that Gilson's analysis of our *postmodern* predicament has been told, what does he offer us in the way of a solution? Precisely the sort of advice we would expect from a true and serious philosopher. He admonishes us that we will not find the remedy for our predicament by wallowing in *postmodernity's* evil. We will find it by courageously seeking and attacking its *metaphysical and moral causes*. "Let us not say: it is too late, and there is nothing left to do; but let us have the courage to look for the evil and the remedy where they exist." (29)

Since "falsely-so-called" *postmodernity's* chief problem is that we have lost reason (logos) in touch with reality because we have lost God, Gilson tells us, our solution is simple. We will not find our reason and recover touch with reality again until we have "first found God again." And we will not find God again without the willingness "to receive what still remains of grace today." (p. 29)

To do that, we must turn our souls again to the world, to have them measured by the being of things, not by our unbridled and unmoored poetic imaginations. Beyond this, we add, *we must first recognize that we are rational animals possessed of immortal souls!*

To do all this, as Gilson understood, we must attempt once again to inhabit the universe of St. Thomas in which the service of God and reason are compatible and produce in us order, beauty, and joy—not nausea—because, in this world, unlike the insane, postmodern Enlightenment world, the necessary condition for the existence of one does not entail the necessary destruction of the other. For, sharing the same cause as part of the same creation, the order of our freedom, thoughts, and reality complement, they do not contradict, one another.

By submitting the measure of our souls to the being of things (which, as a practical matter, for Gilson and us, simultaneously entails implicit recognition of God's existence), Gilson knew we would have some hope of recovering our common sense and sanity and avoiding modernity's/*postmodernity's* slaughterhouse. We "either serve Him in spirit and in truth," Gilson admonishes us, "or we shall enslave ourselves ceaselessly, more and more, to the monstrous idol which we have made with our own hands to our image and likeness." (9–31)

In so doing, we need to recall Gilson's admonition that we human beings think the way we can, not the way we wish. Analogously, this applies to the way we imagine, judge, understand, and reason. In signing on to this Manifesto, its signatories are chiefly opposing the principles presently being applied in sometimes good and sometimes bad faith by different people—causes which might produce effects that, *when abstractly considered*, might appear to them to be, and might even be, logically consistent; but, which, *when applied to reality* in an individual situation, time and place, can never generate a really doable deed by this or that person or group.

Abstract conceptual non-contradictions very often wind up being real contradictions that cannot cause the intended actions we seek when we try to execute them in reality. As a result, sometimes those who appear to be our best friends wind up being our worst enemies; and sometimes those who appear to be our worst enemies actually become our best friends. For this reason, we welcome civil and constructively intended criticism of any of the points we have made in this Manifesto and in the tactical principles we articulate below to realize its strategic ends.

This Manifesto's Principles of Action to Counteract Growing Political Totalitarianism, Its Denial of Civil Liberties, Natural Moral Law, and Its Disrespect for Natural Human Rights and Human Dignity

A Brief Historical Report of the Polish Solidarity Movement as a Preamble to the Tactical Principles of the GCSU

In reaction to just the sort of totalitarian world situation that Adler, Merton, Lewis, and Gilson had described above, several decades ago the Polish people sought to liberate themselves from the Totalitarian Gulag to which, for decades, they had been subjected to live, this Manifesto seeks to articulate in what follows principles for a practical plan of action analogously, on a global scale, to imitate the Polish Solidarity Movement model that worked to help restore an increase of civil rights in Poland toward the end of the twentieth century.

Formally founded on 22 September 1980 when delegates of 36 regional trade unions met in Gdańsk (previously the Free City of Danzig), the now world-famous Polish *Solidarity* trade union (STU) organized itself under its Polish name: *Solidarność*. In so doing, the STU became the first independent labor union in a Soviet bloc nation.

During a growing wave of new strikes in 1980 protesting rising food prices, under the leadership of Lech Wałesa, the Lenin Shipyards in Gdańsk became an organized center of resistance to government *mandates* after approximately 17,000 workers had organized a strike and barricaded themselves within the plant. Shortly after this, in mid-August, 1980, the STU helped organized an Inter-factory Strike Committee (ISC) to help coordinate *rapidly spreading strikes* in different locations at a short notice.

By early 1981, the STU had about 10 million members and represented most of Poland's workers; and before the end of August of the same year, the ISC had presented the Polish government with a list of demands in the form of a Charter of Workers' Rights

(CWR). On August 31, the government and the Gdańsk strikers had reached an agreement allowing the existence of "free and independent unions with the right to strike, together with greater freedom of religious and political expression."

Throughout the remaining few months of 1981, *Solidarity* organized against the Soviet-controlled government led by General Wojciech Jaruzelski by engaging in increasingly stronger, more numerous, controlled strikes, immediately followed by increasing demands for economic reforms and increased civil liberties—including free elections and trade-union involvement in highest-level, national, political decision making. Under growing pressure from his Soviet overlords to gain political control over the situation in Poland, in a bid to crush the Solidarity movement, on 13 December 1981, Jaruzelski's government: (1) imposed martial law nationally; (2) declared *Solidarity* illegal; (3) arrested its leaders. On October 8, 1982, it had the Polish Parliament (the Sejm) formally dissolve the STU.

Nonetheless, for seven years *Solidarity* remained in existence as an underground organization and opposition political movement. In 1989, *Solidarity* led a new wave of coordinated strikes and labor unrest across Poland. Among the strikers' major demands was government recognition of *Solidarity*. In April 1989, the government agreed to legalize *Solidarity* and allow it to participate in free elections to a bicameral Polish parliament. While *Solidarity's* political influence thereafter diminished, this was only because the STU had helped Poles recover previously lost civil liberties and give birth to a multitude of new political parties. (For more about the Polish Solidarity Movement, see: https://www.britannica.com/summary/Solidarity.)

Tactical Principles of the GCSU

1. The signatories and affiliate organizations involved in cooperating to generate this historic, Global Renaissance Manifesto present this history of the Polish *Solidarity Movement* as a model of the following commonsense political principles for us to apply and

emulate in our own day so as to reverse the increasingly growing power, and numbers, of totalitarian political governments coming into being worldwide.

2. These signatories and affiliate organizations agree to send this Manifesto to, and ask to support our cause, the following:

A. National and international leaders of different unions and organizations who have refused to cave into Covid-19 mandates—like hospital workers, airline workers, police, firefighters, military, religious, and so on—and ask them to sign on to this manifesto, tell their membership about it, and ask them to join us, become a member of GCSU.

B. Talented writers and speakers, philosophers, theologians, poets: liberal artists of different sorts who know how to recognize, and use their talent to fight, propaganda and support our cause.

C. Politicians and people with political influence who agree with our principles and are willing to support our work.

D. Journals, periodicals, and media outlets of different kinds to spread our message.

E. Any person or organization we can think of who might be able to assist us in our efforts.

3. These signatories and affiliate organizations also further agree to cooperate:

A. To create a GCSU website, an international board of directors and board of advisors from as many professional fields, countries, as possible. The board should have solid scholars from several disciplines—including: medicine/biology/virology and the like, including religious leaders and clergy from all over the world.

B. To include within this website the following:

(1) a place where other scholars and other professionals and supporters can sign the Manifesto;

(2) a section with useful material divided by discipline and topics (philosophy, theology, law, medicine, virology, epidemiology,

etc.; adverse effects, overall mortality rate, green pass policies, human rights violations, early treatments, etc.);

(3) a division section for scholarly articles;

(4) an international news page from different countries with at least one associate editor from each country) with key news and links to like-minded, and not-so-like-minded groups/associations

(5) even if only for cultural purposes, a page with information about the Nuremberg trial, to be composed over the next few years, to help show the long-term effects of the present Covid-19 madness and help prevent this insanity from ever happening again;

C. To create a quarterly online Journal/Review, and perhaps an annual hard copy of the quarterly articles.

D. If possible, to involve a charitable organization to help secure donations for us so that we might be soon in a position to pay collaborators and website maintenance.

E. To form a group of GCSU Fellows and Senior Fellows to publish newspaper editorials and give radio, TV, and blogsite interviews; and perhaps develop our own media in these areas.

F. To establish a fund of some kind to help: 1) police, firefighters, military members, and others who put conscience and the public good first; and 2) members of the general public whose health has been damaged through vaccine mandates and/or forced vaccination.

G. To establish an online *Global Commonsense University* rooted in the uncommon commonsense philosophical principles that we have reported and in this Manifesto to: 1) replace the failed Enlightenment colleges and universities whose professors have been a chief cause of the cultural mess in which we currently find ourselves; 2) produce future world leaders with the uncommon commonsense wisdom and prudence that the world sorely needs today and will need tomorrow.

H. Finally, to establish within this University an International Humanist Center for Global Leadership and World Peace led by our faculty, students, and graduates.

A Philosophical Call To Renew American Culture: The Homeschool Renaissance

Peter A. Redpath, Ph.D.

Today, nationally and globally, America is at a crossroad.[1] We face daunting educational and political problems. No social order born of a common conviction in the truth and goodness of its principles can long survive when it cannot rationally justify this conviction. At this historical moment, a critical meltdown is occurring in American educational and political institutions because, increasingly, the general American population and our institutional leaders cannot rationally justify the truth and goodness of the principles upon which our American educational and political institutions depend for their survival and health.

During the twentieth century, totalitarian political systems externally threatened the American democratic concept. In the face of these systems, America generally defended itself through a combination of physical force, free market competition, pragmatic arguments about the superiority of the American way of life, and the moral conviction of the American people about the just nature of

---

1   This, and the following essay, are re-published courtesy of The Angelicum Academy. Both essays comprise a Commonsense Manifesto responding to the SDS "Port Huron Statement/Manifesto originally penned by Tom Hayden. The original articles may be found here: https://www.angelicum.net/classical-homeschooling-magazine/first-issue/a-philosophical-call-to-renew-american-culture-the-homeschool-renaissance/

their cause and the goodness of their society. At this time in our history, while we still have external enemies, America faces another, more pernicious, internal threat, that we cannot defeat through physical force, the free market, or pragmatic slogans about the superiority of the American way of life: the inability rationally to justify the truth and moral goodness of American society.

Educationally, sophistry reigns supreme in America today. Since 1983, millions of Americans have reached high school senior year without learning the basics of reading, mathematics, and U.S. history. Millions of teenagers have dropped out of high school.[2] Today, an average student, even at better American colleges and universities, cannot think abstractly or read a difficult book without individual proctoring.[3]

Many faculty members are illiterate, and, especially in the social sciences, cannot explain the nature of their subject matter, the method their discipline uses, the origin of their principles, or what makes their principles scientific. The State arbitrarily undermines parental authority in favor of "enlightened" social causes. Our public schools cannot teach the philosophical and moral principles that sustain the authority of our political institutions. These schools are crime-ridden. We have reached a point in public education where we cannot agree on curricula, especially in areas of history, ethics, and politics. We are graduating increasing numbers of illiterate students, often warehoused for years by incompetent teachers. Yet our most successful politicians tend to graduate from, and send their children to, private schools.

In politics, we increasingly remove moral principles and truth from the domain of public life. Irrationally and sophistically, we identify the sphere of public life with the secular realm, and justice with the domain of the Machiavellian will-of-the-stronger. Often,

---

[2] "A Nation at Risk," in *Policy Review*, 90 (July/August 1998) 23-24.
[3] Mortimer J. Adler noted this problem as far back as 1940. See Mortimer J. Adler, *How to Read a Book: The Art of Getting a Liberal Education*, New York: Simon and Schuster, Inc., 1940) 11.

we judge deceit, selfishness, and subordination of the common good in order to win political office, as hallmarks of wisdom.

States come into being through, are the creation of, other mediating institutions, like families, churches, synagogues, schools, private businesses, and so on. Collections of individuals do not found States as collective wills to which we become serfs. Through representatives, people, as social beings (with skills and factional interests), and as moral agents (with natural rights and duties), and members of communities, establish States as limited, mediating agencies, through which we self-govern ourselves in pursuit of our common good: the more perfect union we achieve through political peace and justice.

The notion of limited government did not begin with modernity or the European Enlightenment. Moses adhered to this principle in his dealings with Pharaoh. The ancient Greeks recognized this principle in their articulation of the four cardinal moral virtues: prudence, justice, temperance, and courage. And St. Thomas Aquinas, referring to St. Augustine, explicitly appeals to this principle in his treatment of the variety of human law in Question 91 of I-II of his *Summa Theologiae*.[4]

Principally and primarily, the State is a peace officer, not a parent, nurturer, clothier, guardian, educator, nor chief economist. The proper subject of State governance is human freedom. States exist because human freedom exists. States exist to regulate human freedom within the bounds of justice and State competence in order to promote the common good of civic peace and friendship. States exist principally and primarily to regulate human freedom in relation to human exchanges, to maintain peace and order within these exchanges. They do not exist principally and primarily to es-

---

4   Peter A. Redpath, "What's Wrong with Government Schools?", in *Social Justice Review* 89 (November/December, 1998) no. 11-12, 164. St. Thomas Aquinas, *Summa Theologiae*, I-II, q. 91, a.4, respondeo. See, also, Plato, *Republic*, Bk. 1, 334C-354B, and *Gorgias*, 491D-500D.

tablish and operate schools, or to run motels, real estate agencies, businesses, hospitals, or restaurants.[5]

States come into being because we human beings have a natural desire, and a moral obligation, to pursue our own happiness through exercise of our choices. To pursue our happiness, we must exercise our freedom. To exercise freedom, we need conducive circumstances. The State exists principally and primarily as a peace officer to facilitate the circumstances under which we can justly exercise our political freedom.[6]

Freedom is proper to man's nature. In our actions, we have a moral right to exercise our freedom virtuously relative to our personal welfare, and a political right to exercise it justly relative to the common good.

The principal right to reward people for virtue and punish them for vice lies with God, not individual human beings, or the State. Hence, in our dealings with others, we have to be cautious not to overstep the bounds of our moral authority. God has the moral authority to command and reward all acts of virtue and to punish all vice. Individual human beings do not. God's moral authority prohibits all human evils. Individual moral authority only extends to communities over which individuals can exercise competent judgment and influence. For human beings, the domain of any moral authority is always the sphere of the humanly possible relative to some human good. No one, including States or God, has a right to command the impossible, which is what States do when they overextend their authority.

As parents, we cannot outlaw all wrongdoing by our children, and we cannot justly command of them impossible acts of virtue. As human beings, children have a right to exercise their freedom within the bounds of justice and household peace. When they overstep these bounds, parents have a moral right to punish them.

---

[5] Redpath, "What's Wrong with Government Schools?", 164.
[6] Ibid.

Similarly, in the political domain, private morality is the dimension of human freedom related to the pursuit of personal welfare, inasmuch as this has no detrimental impact on civic peace and friendship. From a political perspective, in our private lives, we have a moral jurisdiction that allows us to be as intemperate, cowardly, foolish, and unjust as we please in our dealings with others, until our actions start to undermine civic peace and friendship. The domain of public morality, from which we derive our public moral principles, should not be merely the dimension of secular behavior – the arena of a public secular religion, where only secular reason has a right to speak and where truth is measured by an "enlightened" intellectual elite and governmental bureaucrats.[7]

While many people derive their moral principles from religion, others do not. Many people, such as atheists and agnostics, derive their moral principles from personal experience at living, from tradition, or from philosophy. Other people derive their moral principles from revelation. To demand that such people adopt a secular religion before they can enter political debate that involves a common good to which they contribute and common threats by which they are endangered violates human and Constitutional rights to freedom for religion and speech.

Essentially, morality has two domains: our duties toward other people and our duties toward God. Religion is a moral obligation we have toward God. As such, it presupposes, it does not essentially generate, moral principles. God, not religion, is the source of moral principles. God imbeds these principles in human nature, in the voice of conscience, and freely gives this voice to theists, atheists, and agnostics. Religion arises as a reaction in some people to the voice of conscience. The voice of conscience does not arise as an act of religion.

---

7   Peter A. Redpath, "Private Morality and Public Enforcement," in Curtis L. Hancock and Anthony O. Simon, eds., *Freedom, Virtue, and the Common Good* (Notre Dame, Ind.: American Maritain Association, distributed by University of Notre Dame Press, 1995) pgs. 332-341.

To claim that religion, not God, is essentially the source of morality is a major fallacy of the Enlightenment. It implies that atheists and agnostics are essentially devoid of conscience, are not moral agents, an assertion contradicted by much historical experience. Submission of conscience to the rule of justice imbedded in human inclinations authorizes citizens to have a public voice. This rule of justice relative to the common good, not submission to a secular religion, generates the authority of civil law. The rule of justice relative to the common good, not submission to a secular religion, is the standard of political tolerance. To demand that our right to participate in public moral discourse rests upon adoption of a secular religion and its secularized rules of tolerance violates natural human rights, the American Constitution, and American pluralism.

Public morality is the domain of freedom involving personal exchanges that impact on the common good of civic peace and friendship: the domain of civic justice and public safety. As soon as a human action enters this arena, it passes from morally private to morally public jurisdiction, the arena of public safety regulable by just, not unlimited, tolerance. In this arena, all citizens have a right to a public voice. In this domain, moral responsibility and irresponsibility impact on all citizens regardless of religious or non-religious affiliation. In this arena, the domain of justice and freedom, where human actions impact upon our common good and threaten us with common dangers:

(1) all human beings, by natural possession of a conscience, are competent judges and have a natural right to speak; and,

(2) justice, relative to the common good, establishes the limits of tolerance. Here, the voice of conscience, philosophy, personal experience, and religious traditions all have something to contribute.

Philosophy and the Common Good

For several decades, through increasing identification of the State with the Body Politic, and sophistic appeal to the secularly religious grounds of the State's public morality, we have steadily diminished parental authority over the education of children and decreased the public voice of ordinary citizens, religious leaders, and classical philosophers in political debates that affect our common good and public welfare. The net result of this effort has been an increasing erosion of American educational and political institutions.

Like every constitutional political order, American society came into being through a conventional agreement made by representatives of political factions to unite in the pursuit of a common political good, a more perfect political union. The American government did not create this political vision of the common good. The government's existence presupposed, and arose from, this common goal articulated in the Constitution. The American government exists to preserve, protect, and defend this common good and the principles that sustain it.

The American vision of the common good is historically rooted in Western philosophical and theological convictions about human nature and destiny that the American founders considered to be self-evident. Without familiarity with these convictions, we cannot grasp the nature or meaning of our political institutions and political lives.

We become like strangers wandering amidst foreign and unfamiliar surroundings. We erroneously start to believe that our own self-definition grounds our freedom and political principles.

Central to the Western vision of the common good is a philosophical conviction about the fundamental rationality and dignity of human nature and the theological conviction that human life is guided by a providential creator. The major ancient Greek philosophers never deviated in their judgment that our universe is an intelligible order inhabited by a gradation of beings, each with its own non-relative identity, culminating in human nature, a social animal endowed with the faculty to reason.

The ancient Greek philosophers thought we were born with the natural ability to survey the physical world around us and to extract from our everyday observations of the behavior of physical things the rules whereby we develop our arts, sciences, morals, law, and politics. For these philosophers, inclinations in this organic faculty of reason, whereby we moderate our use of freedom in pursuit of our own welfare and act with reasonable tolerance toward others, constitute the voice of reason – conscience – the locus of the universal moral principles that determine moral normalcy. They thought that to ignore, or to behave contrary to, reason's dictates was vicious, made us less human and more beastly, and eventually led to our emotional, intellectual, and social corruption.[8]

Medieval Jewish, Muslim, and Christian thinkers inherited and preserved the Greek philosophical view of nature, the arts, and sciences, and built around them our Western cultural, educational, theological, legal, and political traditions. For several centuries, but especially within the past several decades, the ancient Greek understanding of philosophy and human nature has decreased in some of these traditions. Wherever this has occurred, disaster has resulted. Philosophy is the only rational knowledge by which we can judge the principles of demonstration in our arts and sciences, evaluate the worth of our knowledge, identify and evaluate our criteria of truth, distinguish sound from unsound arguments, and unify our sciences into an order of higher learning. And philosophical reflection upon the behavior of human beings, understood as rational animals, is the only means we have to establish a rationally justified ethics and a concept of the person that can sustain democratic government.

Democratic government presupposes a specific vision of the common human good. And our concept of a common human good necessarily contains our concept of human nature. Democratic government is a type of government naturally best suited for achieving the common good of rational animals, not of irra-

---

8   Etienne Gilson, *The Unity of Philosophical Experience* (New York: Charles Scribner's Sons, 1965) 272-293. Peter A. Redpath, "The New World Disorder: A Crisis of Philosophical Identity," in *Contemporary Philosophy*, 16 (November/December 1994) no. 6, 19-24.

tional animals or angels. Totalitarianism suits beasts. Theocracy befits angels.

At present, we Americans find ourselves in a state of educational and political decay because we have lost our understanding of the nature of classical philosophy and the essential role it plays in integrating all our branches of knowledge, our cultural and political institutions, in justifying our common vision of our common political good, and rationally articulating the jurisdictional lines of private and public morality. Having lost our understanding of the nature of this subject, we can no longer find rational arguments to justify and sustain our different educational and religious institutions and the principles that sustain us in our common convictions about our common good. The existence of these institutions essentially depends upon, and can only be rationally justified by, philosophical arguments that presuppose that we are rational animals. Having lost this conviction, we have lost our ability to think philosophically. Thus, we can no longer rationally justify American culture.

Transmission of the principles that justify a culture's vision of the common good is the work of theologians and philosophers. American culture is theologically pluralistic. For this reason alone, it can never theologically justify a unified vision of the democratic common good to its own people, much less to people of different theological traditions who would attack America externally.

Since its inception, America has attempted to use a lowest common biblical tradition as a kind of public philosophy to justify the intellectual and moral norms that sustain our common democratic vision. Given the common Judeo-Christian and European tradition of previous generations of Americans, rhetorical appeal to such a common theological tradition was possible to sustain our way of life. Growing American pluralism and secularization no longer make this possible.

Having weakened our theological traditions, we largely only have sophistry, empty slogans, to justify our cultural, educational, and political institutions. No democracy can rationally sustain itself on sophistic principles. For this reason, our schools have lost their ability to teach, our universities are gradually being transformed into propaganda institutes, and our politicians increasingly think that words mean whatever they want them to mean.

Philosophy is not a lowest common theology, a secular religion from which we get our public morality, or any specific system or body of knowledge. It is a method of rational investigation that involves use of sense observation, abstract conceptualization, and logical reasoning, a natural mode of higher-level inquiry employed by human beings, rational animals. This understanding of human nature and philosophy is common to our Western theological traditions and to ordinary human beings in all parts of the world. And it was the general understanding that prevailed in the West when universities first arose during the Middle Ages.

Some Immediate Steps to Take

Universities are the main source from which America draws its institutional leaders. If America's universities are intellectually and morally weak, American institutions will not long remain intellectually and morally strong. America's universities are intellectually and morally weak. Hence, American institutions cannot long remain intellectually and morally strong.

Currently, philosophy is required at perhaps, no more than twenty-five percent of American colleges and universities. Even at those schools that require philosophy, what passes for philosophy is often sophistry, having little resemblance to the mode of abstract reasoning that the ancient Greeks considered to be natural to rational animals. The decline of classical philosophy at our universities helps explain the widespread inability of contemporary American college students to think abstractly, reason logically, maintain their attention span, distinguish sound from fallacious arguments, and read difficult books.

A morally vicious and intellectually gullible citizenry cannot sustain democratic government. Loss of our ability to reason well corrupts our democratic institutions, places them in the hands of sophists, and makes us dupes to the persuasive force of ideological slogans and sound bites. We cannot turn to contemporary social scientists, psychologists, political and cultural theorists, literary critics, or contemporary philosophers to remedy our current educational, cultural, and political problems. Generally, their theories are the sophistry that lie at the source of our decay. To seek help from them resembles asking incendiaries to fight a forest fire.[9]

To renew our nation, we must renew our institutions. To renew our institutions, we must renew our universities. To renew our universities, we need a renaissance of classical philosophical and theological education, from the ground up as well as from the top down. The huge and growing "homeschooling" movement presents an opportunity to initiate this classical philosophical and theological educational renaissance, starting in the elementary and secondary levels and then reaching into the colleges and universities.

Homeschoolers heavily favor those colleges where classical philosophical and theological education still exists (for example, the student body of Thomas Aquinas College is now about 30% homeschooled). These colleges, especially those with a component of traditional theology, are rapidly expanding. Homeschooling is increasing at a rate of approximately 15% per year. Already, competition for these students is exerting tremendous pressure on college administrations to hire faculty and alter their curricula in that direction. This trend will doubtlessly increase.

Many universities, which previously shunned homeschoolers, now actively recruit them. New colleges geared toward homeschoolers and their traditional and classical yearnings are already

---

9 Peter A. Redpath, "Dirty Dancing: Higher Education as Enlightened Swindling," in Peter A. Redpath, *Masquerade of the Dream Walkers: Prophetic Theology from the Cartesians to Hegel* (Amsterdam and Atlanta: Editions Rodopi, B.V., 1998). I thank Curtis L. Hancock for calling my attention to this simile.

on the drawing boards (for example, Patrick Henry College, The Great Books University College, Yorktown University). We need to encourage this trend.

Western culture and theological traditions inherited their philosophical principles from the ancient Greek conviction that the world is intelligible to unaided natural reason and that the highest form of human education lies in becoming an independent learner. The Delphic oracle's prescription to "know thyself" captures the motivating principle behind the ancient Greek pursuit of philosophy. As Socrates well understood, principally and primarily, all learning is self-teaching.

To become highly educated, we must facilitate this self-teaching through apprenticeship with great discoverers (of being, truth, unity, goodness, and beauty) and tutoring from masters of the liberal arts of learning: those people who can challenge us to develop the discipline whereby we can acquire the principles for reading great books. In this way, we can enter into conversation with the great discoverers, most of whom are long dead. Hopefully, through life-long conversation with these great intellects, we can ourselves become independent learners and great discoverers, and can pass on to posterity the principles that sustain our culture, those discovered and taught by the great discoverers and teachers of the past and set down in their great books, including Scriptural texts.

Unhappily, public, and most private, education in the United States today inverts the classical order of learning. Our public and private educational systems have lost the Greek understanding that the first and most essential teacher is the student, next comes the great discoverer, and last comes the classroom teacher, whose main task should be to help students learn the liberal art of reading difficult classic books. It should not be to masquerade as a great discoverer oneself. As Mortimer J. Adler is fond of saying, "A classroom teacher is only a better student."

Homeschooling, as most homeschooled students soon discover, is, after the first few years of coaching in the liberal arts (which are best taught one-on-one – hence at home), very largely self-teaching. If we equate self-teaching with the current practical expression of that concept, homeschooling, we can see that the ancient Greeks well understood what our culture is being forced to concede reluctantly: all learning is essentially self-teaching. The superior academic performance of homeschoolers, now widely known and admitted, provides objective evidence of this fact. We best encourage and support self-teaching by preparing students for, and guiding them to, the classic works of the great discoverers, at home, close to the loving arms of parents, who are more likely to be able to give them the one-to-one tutoring attention that professional educators constantly tell us is essential to maximizing student achievement.

Genuine higher education (in the sense of developing the higher intellectual virtues such as understanding and wisdom, and not just the memory) begins when we start to take control over our self-teaching, when we no longer need an auxiliary teacher's help to discover the principles by which to learn. Contemporary public and private educational systems largely invert and undermine this classical view of learning and higher education. While they often give lip-service to developing independent learners, and one-to-one tutoring, the educational practices they employ actually do the opposite: cripple the ability of students to think abstractly and become self-teachers.

Our educational institutions have largely abolished the Socratic method of using discussions and disputations among student-learners to encourage abstract thinking and deepen understanding of difficult and lofty concepts, traditionally called the "Great Ideas." Thus, secondary educational institutions neglect the one area that might be especially helpful to us for promoting abstract thought, higher education, and independent learning. More than any other institutions, our contemporary public and private educational systems sustain and propagate the sophistic educational mindset that has undermined the Greek educational vision that, for centuries, has supported Western culture and our democratic republic. To overturn this mindset, we must restore the classical view that learning is chiefly accomplished by homeschooling (that is, self-teaching) with the help of the great discoverers.

At this juncture in American history, homeschooling (especially classical homeschooling, leading to the study of Western civilization's great books), and efforts to develop ways to support the secondary liberal education of homeschoolers (including the organization of Socratic discussion groups) is one of our best hopes to halt our culture's decline. These homeschoolers now stream into our universities. Soon they will flood them. In my opinion, this is the irrepressible wave of the future. This Homeschool Renaissance may well be the West's last, large-scale, educational reform movement, and so our nation's best practical hope to halt what others have called this twilight of civilization from fading into another Dark Age of ignorance and chaos.

The Homeschool Renaissance And The Battle Of The Arts[1]

Peter A. Redpath, Ph.D.

In the inaugural issue of *Classical Homeschooling* magazine, I issued a homeschool manifesto, a philosophical call, to renew American culture through a homeschool renaissance.[2][3] At the start of the "Prologue" to a little treatise that he wrote around the age of thirty, St. Thomas Aquinas warns his readers that, according to Aristotle, small mistakes in the beginning eventually become large mistakes in the end.[4] Such being the case, prudence dictates that, as we initiate this homeschool renaissance, we avoid making initial errors. To do this, prudence also dictates that we call upon historical experience.

Thus, to help us avoid initial mistakes, and to establish our renaissance on a solid foundation, a good place for us to start our work is from a study of beginnings of the last great Western Renaissance, the

Italian Renaissance of the fourteenth century. When we do this, we find a time dominated by a peculiar intellectual spirit that conflated poetry, rhetoric, and theology, one increasingly anti-philosophical and anti-Scholastic. We commonly identify the start of

---

1   Original publication of this essay may be found here: https://www.angelicum.net/classical-homeschooling-magazine/first-issue/a-philosophical-call-to-renew-american-culture-the-homeschool-renaissance/
2   Note: Such a conference was held on June 1 & 2, 2001 in Lawrence, KS by *Classical Homeschooling* magazine.
3   Peter A. Redpath, "A Philosophical Call to Renew American Culture: The Homeschool Renaissance," in *Classical Homeschooling*, Summer 2000, 23-38.
4   St. Thomas Aquinas, *On Being and Essence*, trans. Armand A. Maurer (Toronto: Pontifical Institute of Mediaeval Studies), 28.

this Renaissance with the Italian humanist Francesco Petrarcha, Petrarch (1304-1374). Paul Oskar Kristeller is generally recognized as the twentieth-century's leading historian of Renaissance thought. Kristeller tells us that reading ancient Latin writers and seeing Rome's ancient monuments evoked in Petrarch and many other Italian humanists a strong nostalgia for the political greatness of the Roman Republic and Empire and that the central idea that guided Petrarch in his dealings with the Pope and political figures was hope to restore this greatness.[5]

Kristeller's point is that, at least in part, a political project motivated the Italian Renaissance's growth: the desire to restore the political greatness of Roman culture. At least three things are crucial to understand to comprehend this project: (1) it first arose within the nostalgic minds and wills of Italian humanists, (2) it caused certain humanists to develop an apocryphal notion of philosophy that identified the birth of philosophy with the Israelites, not the Greeks, and, especially, with Moses, and (3), Kristeller reports that, before student slang coined the term "humanist" during the fifteenth century, humanists were usually known by the name "poets", although many of them would hardly deserve the label by modern standards. This notion also may help us to understand why the defense of poetry, one of the favorite topics of early humanist literature, involved a defense of humanist learning as a whole.

No less important than poetry was the humanist study of rhetoric or oratory, and again the "humanists" were very often identified as orators, or as poets and orators, before the term humanist had come into use.[6]

Desire to rebuild Roman political greatness by restoring Roman culture in a new and better Christian version had motivated Italian humanists to read classical poets and rhetoricians. In Chris-

---

5   Paul Oskar Kristeller, *Eight Philosophers of the Italian Renaissance* (Stanford: Standord University Press, 1964), 7.
6   Peter A. Redpath, *Wisdom's Odyssey from Philosophy to Transcendental Sophistry* (Amsterdam and Atlanta: Editions Rodopi, 1997), 72 and 86-125.

tian culture during Petrarch's time, poetry lacked the prestige of the other liberal arts. Medieval schools often studied poetry, like history, as part of rhetoric, generally as a mode of composition within rhetoric called the "art of letter writing" (ars dictaminis).[7] "So considered, no separate division of poetry existed within the Medieval liberal arts curriculum."[8] And many people viewed suspiciously any reading of pagan poets because pagan poets had been idolaters and polytheists who portrayed the gods in morally negative terms.[9] Petrarch's project had a serious obstacle to overcome. To transcend the pagan poets the humanists had to read them.

To overcome this obstacle, Charles Trinkhaus indicates that humanists started to assert "the importance of form and style" to replace "the older *trivium* and *quadrivium* as preliminary studies to theology, law or medicine," and "to end the elevation of dialectic and the downgrading of grammar, rhetoric and poetry in the Arts faculties of the universities."[10] Thanks to the efforts of Petrarch and fellow Italian humanists, by the fifteenth century, school documents and library classification schemes indicate the studia humanitatis had usurped the classical understanding of the liberal arts by removing logic from the trivium and adding poetry, history, and moral philosophy, to constitute a new discipline of the humanities divided into five parts: grammar, rhetoric, poetry, history, and ethics.[11]

Starting with Petrarch, Italian humanists began to allegorize and figuratively interpret classical Greek philosophy and Western history, and they revived an apocryphal version of the origin of philosophy initially fabricated by Alexandrian Jewish apologists as far back as the second century B.C. Humanists commonly maintained that philosophy is an inspired, esoteric system of revelation, a lofty metaphysical and moral doctrine, an original monotheistic religion. Most often they traced the origin of this system to Moses.

7   Ibid., 93.
8   Ibid.
9   Ibid., 95.
10 Ibid., 92-93.
11 Ibid., 93.

They often claimed that idolaters, such as Babylonians, Chaldeans, and Egyptians, had stolen this doctrine from the ancient Israelites, and that ancient poets had hidden this sacred teaching beneath lofty and allegorical language and exceptional individuals such as magi, prophets, priests, and epic poets like Vergil had esoterically transmitted it across the ages. Later humanists, starting with Lorenzo Valla, further maintained that truth lies in original linguistic usage and that this doctrine had been first revealed in an original, ancient language.

More specifically, Petrarch and other humanists: (1) asserted that, to protect their lofty metaphysical and moral truths from the common masses, and confound and inspire awe in the "vulgar," ancient poets fabricated ridiculous, hyperbolic, allegorical stories about gods and heroes that any rational person would recognize as false; (2) used allegorical and figurative interpretation to unravel the true philosophical and Christian theological meaning of poetic works; (3) promoted William of Ockham's nominalistic thesis that nature "occulty" produces universals, or abstract general ideas, in the mind and the nominalist view that the world is a book the meaning of which is wrapped in oracular language; (4) maintained that only someone with a special poetic, or prophetic, gift of revealing concealed meanings can confront these individual, sensible beings and elevate them to the status of universals; and (5) claimed that, over time, pagan philosophers corrupted and passed on to Medieval Christian theologians, principally Scholastics, a counterfeit version of the true system of philosophy. The humanists then united these five elements with a deconstruction of the Scholastic psychological foundations for the sciences and combined this with an attack on Aristotle's teaching about forms.[12]

In short, part of Petrarch's project of reviving Roman political greatness was to conflate poetry, religion, philosophy, and theology to develop a new profession and discipline: the profession of theologizing poets (poetae theologisantes) and the discipline of poetic theology (theologia poetica). Humanists achieved this by

---

12   Ibid., 97-98, 104.

making the object of philosophical knowledge a historical act of revelation and the method for revealing this object a religious act of inspiration and historical transmission. Petrarch thus initiated a general humanist view of philosophy as poetic transmission of religious history.[13]

Clearly, part of the early humanist program was to set the humanities against natural science and Aristotelian logic. It involved more, however: undermining the union of philosophy and Scholastic theology. Early on, therefore, humanists engaged in apologetic defenses of poetry. These are no historical eccentricity. They constitute part of a well-conceived and designed apologetic to elevate poetry's status and diminish the influence of the other liberal arts and philosophy within the university.

As humanists strengthened the identification of poetry with theology, the Medieval view of theology as the queen of the sciences, the stature accorded to the nominalist views of William of Ockham at centers like Oxford and Paris, from which many poets had recently emigrated to Italy, and resort to a centuries-old rhetorical technique of allegorizing other disciplines, coupled with the theological practice of figurative interpretation, helped early humanists solidify the notion of poetry as the divinely-inspired queen of the arts.[14]

As far back as ancient poetry we witness this practice of allegorization of other disciplines in Hesiod's attack on Homer's veracity. The Ionian philosophers extended this attack to include a critique of mythological reasoning as a whole. Plato extended the Ionian attack through allegorization and figurative interpretation of epic poetry, banishment of most of poetry from the ideal city, and removal of the gods from matter and the earth. The Stoics used the same methods to reverse the philosophical onslaught against poetry to the point that Seneca could mockingly remark: "All the schools of philosophy find that their doctrines are in Homer."[15] In late pagan

---

13   Ibid., 96, 103-104.
14   Ibid., 94-95.
15   Ibid., 42.

activity, poets and rhetoricians extended Seneca's attack. By this time, poetry and philosophy became divisions of, and assimilated to, rhetoric. And, by the time of St. Augustine, the notions of rhetor and philosopher were indistinguishable.[16]

Hellenized Jews of the Diaspora and Philo Judaeus further complicated this practice of allegorization and figurative interpretation of other disciplines. Many ancient Greeks tended to portray Jews as cultureless barbarians. Alexandrian Jews reacted against this depiction of them through an apologetic that involved allegorization and figurative interpretation of Greek philosophy. They started to defend the worth of their culture by maintaining that "Greek philosophy owed its origin to the Jewish patriarchs and principally to Moses, who became, to late Judaism, 'the most important figure in the entire history of religion,' the 'true teacher of mankind, the 'superman.'"[17]

Moses and Abraham thus became philosophers. In the second century B. C. Eupolemius wrote: "Moses was the first sage and the first to teach the Jews, and the Greeks from the Phoenicians; and Moses was the first to write laws for the Jews." A couple of centuries later Artapanus claimed that Abraham "taught astrology to the Egyptians and the Phoenicians." He further maintained that Moses was actually Musaeus, Orpheus' teacher, and added: "As a mature man he [Moses] bestowed many things of great use upon mankind. He invented ships and machines for transporting stones, as well as weapons of the Egyptians and machines for irrigation, implements of war, and philosophy."[18]

The famous Jewish philosopher Philo continued this process of allegorization and figurative interpretation of philosophy "by describing Moses as a philosopher and Judaism as the source of philosophy."[19] The Christian apologists Clement and Origen passed on this apocryphal history of philosophy to Sts. Ambrose

---

16   Ibid.
17   Ibid., 43.
18   Ibid.
19   Ibid.

and Augustine. Augustine conflated the notions of liberal arts, music, philosophy, and rhetoric, and, like Ambrose, he justified the study of pagan culture as right and proper expropriation of personal Christian possessions. In his treatise On Christian Doctrine, Augustine went so far as to maintain that "Plato probably learned about Jewish revelation when he had travelled to Egypt and that whatever the Platonists say which is 'good and truthful' they took from the Israelites."[20]

The crucial point to note from this short excursion into ancient and early Medieval history is that, starting with Petrarch, Italian humanists attempted to elevate the status of the disciplines of poetry and rhetoric by allegorizing and figuratively interpreting classical Greek philosophy and Western history to revive an apocryphal version of the origin of philosophy that traces itself to antiquity. They coupled this fabrication with the Ockhamist thesis that nature "occulty" produces universals, or abstract general ideas, in the mind and the popular Medieval view that nature is a book. Then they united these elements with a deconstruction of the Scholastic psychological foundations for the sciences and combined this with an attack on Aristotle's teaching about forms.

Scholastic thinkers generally adopted a psychology similar to the one most people do today. They recognized that we have five external senses (touch, taste, smell, hearing, and sight). To these they added four internal senses (imagination, sense memory, a common or synthetic sense, and particular reason or estimative sense), and emotional appetites. They topped these off with an intellect (which they divided into active and passive and to which they attributed theoretical and practical acts of reason), abstract memory, and will. Most of us today do not talk about a synthetic sense and particular reason, but we do recognize that we have some way of sensing that the act of one sense faculty is not the act of another. Scholastics generally attributed this ability to the common, or synthetic, sense. We also recognize that we have some sort of rudimentary ability to sense distances and to sense things as good or bad for us, or

---

20   Ibid., 47.

the ability that Scholastics attributed to particular reason or the estimative sense. Finally, we recognize that we have an abstractive intellectual ability, an ability to extract general meanings from individual observations, and that this ability is different from our ability to think about things just for the sake of thinking (theoretical reasoning) or to think about things for the sake of doing or making something (practical reasoning).

To deconstruct the Scholastic psychological foundations for the sciences, the humanists confounded the notions of the human imagination, the practical intellect, and the agent intellect. In Scholastic thought, the agent intellect acts as the mediator between mind and the world by abstracting universals, general ideas, from sense images. To elevate poetry over classical philosophy, humanists intentionally confounded the notions of imagination and practical reason and identified both these notions with poetry. They replaced the act of intellectual abstraction with the poetic act of imagination, thereby making poetry mediator between the human senses and the abstract general ideas that act as the ground of all knowing and science. Further to support their project, they promoted the notion that abstract general ideas are occult beings, quasi-magical and largely inert entities that lie prefigured beneath the surface of the material world. As Trinkhaus indicates, Petrarch deliberately initiated a program of locating universals as hidden beneath surface meaning or, through appeal to divine inspiration, infused sacred meaning into a poet's work. Humanists also promoted the notion that the world is a book wrapped in oracular language, identified truth with original linguistic usage, and maintained that only someone with a special poetic, or prophetic, gift of revealing concealed meanings can confront these individual, sensible beings and elevate them to the status of universals.[21]

In short, part of Petrarch's project of reviving Roman political greatness was to develop a new profession and discipline: the profession of theologizing poets (poetae theologisantes) and the discipline of poetic theology (theologia poetica). Crucial to de-

---

21   Ibid., 96.

velopment of this new profession and discipline was a means of conflating poetry, religion, philosophy, and theology. Humanists achieved this by making the object of philosophical knowledge an act of revelation and the method for revealing this object a religious act of inspiration and historical transmission: theological poetry. Petrarch attempts this conflation by maintaining that "To know God, not the gods, is the true and highest philosophy," and that the testimony of Scriptures and Aristotle, who called the first poets "theologizers," "support the contention that theology is simply poetry dealing with God."[22]

The polytheism of the ancient poets and their "depiction of the gods as lustful, envious, fraudulent, duplicitous, mendacious, and so on" presented Petrarch's program with a serious obstacle.[23] He sought to use allegorical and figurative interpretation to overcome these problems. Hence, he maintained that the ancient poets were not polytheists and did not literally accept the portrayal of the gods that they gave. Instead, he claimed the ancient poets were closet monotheists who intentionally depicted the gods in an unbelievable fashion and created the art of poetry and use of hidden meaning to confound, and inspire awe among, the "vulgar."[24] While the "vulgar" might not be able to understand the hidden meaning of ancient poetry, Petrarch maintained that intelligent Christians could recognize the evident absurdities and illusory nature of ancient myth. He also held that the ancient poetic works prefigure Christian revelation which is philosophy's one true teaching.[25] Petrarch thus started a general humanist view of philosophy as poetic transmission of religious history, thereby developing an interest in proper reading of all sorts of ancient religious writings."[26]

Five Renaissance thinkers, especially, refined Petrarch's agenda to conflate poetry, philosophy, true religion, and Jewish and Chris-

---

22 Ibid., 96, 103-104.
23 Ibid., 96.
24 Ibid., 97
25 Ibid., 98.
26 Ibid., 104.

tian theology: Giovanni Boccaccio, Coluccio Salutati, Cristoforo Landino, and Lorenzo Valla, and Marsilio Ficino.

Boccaccio took up Petrarch's mantle by writing a highly influential *Genealogy of the Gods* (*De genealogia deorum*) in which he considered the origins of religion, theology, and poetry. Within the context of this work, Boccaccio maintained that "Moses was the first poet (priscus poetae)," poetry's originator, and poetic and prophetic transmission from the Israelites is the origin of the arts among the gentiles.[27]

Specifically, Boccaccio claimed that religion was originally monotheistic. Noah's descendants corrupted true religion through polytheism, and this corruption reached considerable dimensions around Abraham's time. In preparation for Christ's advent and a return to monotheism, God rose up prophets from among the Israelites, Moses being the most famous. Purportedly, the ancient Greek poets were Moses' historical descendants and prophets who used outward images in their poetry to conceal deeper mysteries. The ancient Greek philosophers depersonified and allegorized Greek myth, thereby further encrusting these theological mysteries in their ideas and technical jargon. As a result, Boccaccio thought that Plato's work contained all of Homer and Judaism.[28]

Salutati extended the identification of true poetry, philosophy, and Judaism by shifting their origin from Moses to Noah's grandson Enoch, who supposedly started them by starting monotheism. Salutati connected pagan poetry's origin to idolatry's origin, which he traced through a crucial passage in Chapter 14 of the *Book of Wisdom*, a reference that will occur repeatedly in humanist and later philosophical writings, including the works of Newton, Kant, and Hegel. According to Salutati's interpretation of the *Book of Wisdom*, idolatry originated from the practice of a grieving father who, on the occasion of his son's death, fashioned an image of his dead son and forced his slaves to hide their true beliefs and worship it. Salutati thought that the pagan poets continued this practice of

---

27   Ibid., 98.
28   Ibid.

hiding their true monotheistic beliefs from public anger under the veil of a double truth and a layer of myths. He also thought that "philosophers are incipient, or prefigured, poets and theologians, because, while the ancient poets intentionally hid their truth behind an eloquent language, the philosophers vulgarized poetic language and did not even comprehend its hidden meaning."[29]

Landino further specified the apocryphal philosophical history started by Petrarch by uniting the notion of theological poet with Platonic theology. Landino argued that poetic knowledge, inspiration, transforms human beings to a semi-divine state, higher than human, not quite a god. This state changes an ordinary human being into a theologian. Supposedly, "the ancient pagan poets incorporated within their work insights from Moses and the prophets. The poets transmitted these revealed truths to the prisci pagan theologians, who transmitted them to Plato."[30]

According to a direct order of transmission, then, Landino maintains, that, in a prefigured form, the works of the ancient poets and philosophers contain the hidden revelation of Christianity, Plato contains the whole of Christian revelation, and, through Plato's influence on Vergil, the greatest ancient poet and philosopher, and Vergil on Dante, Dante has passed on the whole of ancient wisdom to Renaissance poets.[31]

Valla immersed himself in the study of Quintillian's rhetoric with the intention of deconstructing medieval Scholastic philosophy and elevating the status of rhetoric over logic by developing a "theological rhetoric" (*theologia rhetorica*).[32] Valla locates the content of abstract general ideas in original linguistic usage. Purportedly, we find original truth in original historical usage. "For this contains the hidden, or prefigured meaning which transcends the

---

29 Ibid., 98-100
30 Ibid., 102.
31 Ibid., 102-103
32 Ibid., 105.

meaning which exists in books." And original truth grounds all human learning.[33]

Ficino accepted the same sort of fabricated history of philosophy. He thought that the wise and holy men of all nations were priests and philosophers. He claimed that the Hebrew prophets maintained both roles, the Persian philosophers were Magi and priests, Egyptian priests were metaphysicians and mathematicians, Hindu Brahmins studied nature and were priests, and so did the ancient Greek poets and sages, the Celts, Romans, and ancient Christian bishops. Of all religions, he thought that Christianity is the most true because it is the most sincere or pure. He thought that, in creating the world through His Incarnate Word, God the Father sent Fourth into creation in Christ the idea of perfect religion. For Ficino, Christ is a body of knowledge, a repository of divine ideas, including the ideas of perfect religion and incarnate science, underlying the world. Hence, he maintained that Christianity is the origin of all other religions, lying hidden and prefigured underneath them in Christ Incarnate.[34]

Anyone somewhat familiar with the influence of Ficino's Platonic Academy on subsequent thought can readily see how Ficino contributed to transmitting many intellectual errors to subsequent thinkers, including views of deism, a historicist conception that philosophy is a hidden system or body of knowledge, the close identification of the roles of philosopher, poet, priest, and theologian, and the Jewish origin of philosophy. The Italian humanist Polydore Vergil exercised a similar influence through the sixteenth-century publication of a reference book entitled De inventoribus rerum, in which, through the authority of Eusebius and Porphyry, Vergilio traced the origin of philosophy to Moses, from whom the Ionian Thales and the Italian Pythaogras purportedly initiated two new beginnings of philosophy, with the Italian Pythagoras coining the name "philosophy." "Thanks, in part, to the recent invention of the Gutenberg press, Vergilio's work had appeared in thirty Latin

---

33 Ibid., 106.
34 Ibid., 113-118.

THE HOMESCHOOL RENAISSANCE AND
THE BATTLE OF THE ARTS

editions by the time of the author's death in 1555," was "still influential in Leibniz's time," "and by the early eighteenth century more than a hundred versions had accumulated in eight languages, including Russian."[35]

The first authors of modern histories of philosophy, like Thomas Stanley and Georg Horn, were humanist rhetoricians, not philosophers. They continued and solidifed the historical scholarship and "concordist notion that philosophy is revealed, unitary system or body of truth which had been first given directly by God to Moses. They also popularized the claim that this hidden system of knowledge had been later buried in hermetic and cabalist writings and had eventually been passed on through ancient pagan poets up to Plato and beyond."[36]

Had it not been for seventeenth-century attacks against mathematicians in the Jesuit schools and the apologetic efforts of Christopher Clavius, Galileo Galilei and Rene Descartes in defense of mathematicians, this apocryphal notion of philosophy as systematic transmission history, that is, as transmission of a historical system, might have had little connection with modernity. When, however, Renaissance humanists like Benedict Pererius and Alessandro Piccolmini started to attack the reliability of mathematical abstraction and the notion of mathematics as a science, Clavius responded by preparing a disquisition for the Jesuits defending the mathematical disciplines; Galileo answered by observing that, while nature might be a book, because its characters are "triangles, circles and other geometrical figures," the mathematician, not the poet, possesses the method to open it to our gaze, and Descartes replied that while philosophy is a revealed system, it lies buried in the human mind, and Descartes, not Moses, has been the first one to discover it.[37]

---

35 Peter A. Redpath, *Cartesian Nightmare* (Amsterdam and Atlanta: Editions Rodopi, 1997), 7-9.
36 Ibid., 9.
37 Redpath, Wisdom's Odyssey, 89, 103.

In short, while the original humanists like Petrarch would never have intended to give birth to Descartes and modern subjection of the liberal arts to physical science, their politically motivated view of philosophy was elitist, replacing the natural acquisition of science and wisdom through abstract habits of natural reason with dependence on inspiration and historical transmission of hidden teaching through one or another form of language expert.[38]

Renaissance humanism started out as a political project connected to the age-old academic of battle of the liberal arts, a battle that Plato describes in Book 10 of his classic *Republic*. It began by attacking our natural ability to form abstract general ideas and replaced this ability with a poetic act of inspiration. In so doing, it rooted itself in skepticism, superstition, and naive fideism. No wonder, then, that after the Italian Renaissance spent the wealth of Scholastic wisdom and classical philosophy, it generated skepticism, superstition, and blind fideism. Beings act according to their nature.

The great historian of philosophy Etienne Gilson warns us that we think the way we can, not the way we wish. And once we lay down philosophical principles, they develop according to a logic all their own.[39] A small mistake in the beginning winds up being a large mistake in the end. Late Medieval neglect of poetry and rhetoric led Renaissance thinkers like Petrarch, Boccaccio, Landino, Salutati, and Valla to exaggerate the status of these disciplines within the order of human learning and unjustifiably to attack Scholasticism, mathematical learning, and abstraction. This inflationary reaction unwittingly led to the modern identification of all science with mathematics and subjection of our ordinary sense experience of reality, of literary and fine arts, and of philosophy to despotic rule of mathematicism, scientism, and moral relativism.

Educationally and politically, we live in a perilous time. To overcome this peril, we need to free ourselves from the sophistry

---

38   Ibid., 67-68.
39   Etienne Gilson, *Unity of Philosophical Experience* (New York: Charles Scribner's Sons, 1965), 302.

of our age, to transcend the intellectual imperialism to which scientism and moral relativism presently hold our culture hostage, and restore ordinary sense experience, the literary and fine arts, and philosophy to their proper places in the order of human learning. To head in this right direction in this new homeschool renaissance, we need to learn from the mistakes made by the founders of the last great Western Renaissance. We will never accomplish these goals if we confound the orders of learning and ground this renaissance on a renewed battle of the arts. To found this renaissance aright we must cautiously distinguish the orders of learning, identify their natures, and relate them properly. Otherwise, like the last Renaissance, our project will be fated to produce another cycle of skepticism, superstition, and blind fideism. Apart from writing articles in *Classical Homeschooling*, a good way to start such a sound foundation would be through a homeschool conference devoted to the Homeschool Renaissance and the Battle of the Arts. Hopefully, we will see such a conference within the near future.

The Beautiful as a Dimension of Ethics Within the Platonic-Aristotelian Philosophy

Kelly Fitzsimmons Burton, Ph.D.

"Finally, Brothers, whatever is true, whatever is noble, whatever is right, whatever is pure, whatever is lovely, whatever is admirable - if anything is excellent or praiseworthy - think about such things"

Philippians 4:8

Introduction

In the introduction to *What is Art?*, an attempt to interpret Modern conceptions of aesthetic beauty, Leo Tolstoy observes that in the contemporary context:

> A man, a horse, a house, a view, a movement may be beautiful, but of actions, thoughts, character, music, we may say that they are good, if we like them very much, or not good, if we do not like them; we can say 'beautiful' only of what is pleasing to our sight. So that the word and concept 'good' includes within itself the concept 'beautiful', but not vice versa: the concept 'beautiful' does not cover the concept 'good'.[1]

What is noteworthy about this passage is that Modern conceptions of the good include the beautiful, but what is beautiful does not necessarily include the good. What one may consider 'good' is a subjective opinion based upon one's 'likes'. Tolstoy seems to

---

1 Tolstoy, Leo. *What is Art?* (London: Penguin Books; 1995), p.14.

be pointing out a confusion in the Modern context in trying to define beauty when the concept is divorced from any reference to a transcendent good, one that is an objective standard beyond mere opinion. Tolstoy continues: "I will not cite the definitions of beauty ascribed to the ancients - Socrates, Plato, Aristotle, and up to Plotinus - because in fact the concept of beauty separate from the good, which constitutes the basis and aim of aesthetics in our time, did not exist among the ancients".[2] Something has changed in how beauty is conceived in the ancients, and how it is discussed by Modern art theorists. For example, Georg Wilhelm Friedrich Hegel says, in his *Introductory Lectures on Aesthetics*, that:

> ...Art is not, either in content or in form, the supreme and absolute mode of bringing the mind's genuine interests into consciousness ... the spirit of our modern world, or, to come closer, of our religion and our intellectual culture, reveals itself as beyond the stage at which art is the highest mode assumed by man's consciousness of the absolute.[3]

Hegel notes that something about our modern world, religion, or intellectual culture has changed such that "art is, and remains for us, on the side of its highest destiny, a thing of the past. Herein it has further lost for us its genuine truth and life, and rather is transferred into our ideas".[4] Given our historical moment, we now look at art, and I will add, beauty, from an intellectual and analytical point of view. Art and beauty are like artifacts of a previous world and worldview, present to be examined and analyzed, but never again to be re-created. The loss of beauty and fine art in the Modern (and Postmodern) context is due in part to what Charles Taylor describes as the disenchantment of the world. In a summary statement about the transformation in the Modern world from an enchanted to a disenchanted world he says:

---

2   Tolstoy, p.16.
3   Hegel, Georg Wilhelm Friedrich. *Introductory Lectures on Aesthetics* (London: Penguin Books; 2004) p. 12-13.
4   Ibid, p.13.

I have been drawing a portrait of the world we have lost, one in which spiritual forces impinged on porous agents, in which the social was grounded in the sacred and secular time in higher times, in which the play of structure and anti-structure was held in equilibrium; and this human drama unfolded within a cosmos. All this has been dismantled and replaced by something quite different in the transformation we roughly call disenchantment.[5]

Disenchantment, in short, is the loss of a transcendent referent where life is confined to this secular world, or to what Plato will characterize as life in the "Cave". The secularization of modern life, and the loss of a transcendent metaphysical absolute leads to the loss of the ability to look outside the visible world in which we find ourselves in order to produce and appreciate beauty and the beauty of fine art. In addition, without a metaphysical absolute, there is no grounding of the good as the moral absolute. Thus, in the world of disenchantment, we have lost a ground for both the good and the beautiful. We have lost a transcendent source in which to ground both ethics and aesthetics.

In this paper, I will examine the unity between the good and the beautiful in Plato and Aristotle, arguing that the beautiful is an ethical dimension of life related to pursuit of the good. Separation of the beautiful from the good leads to the loss of a transcendental grounding for the beautiful, making beauty merely subjective. In addition, separation of the beautiful and the good from the true leads to skepticism and relativism in ethics and aesthetics. The good for both Plato and Aristotle, is the primary concept in ethics. Virtue is in direct relationship to the good and is a means to the good. Beauty, which partakes in the good, has the features of symmetry, order, harmony, and purity, which apply to aesthetics, but which I will argue are primarily dimensions of ethics, reflecting a life of virtue in pursuit of the good that results in what Plato calls

---

5   Taylor, Charles. *A Secular Age* (Cambridge: Belknap Press of Harvard University Press; 2007), p.61.

a "beautiful soul". In addition to exploring the unity between the good and the beautiful, and arguing for beauty as a dimension of ethics, I will suggest that a reexamination of a Platonic-Aristotelian understanding of the good and the beautiful suggests a means by which to measure a life well-lived, as well as providing a standard for aesthetics in the wake of Tolstoy's observation of the confusion over Modern conceptions of beauty, and in light of Taylor's disenchantment thesis.

The True, The Good, and The Beautiful

In Plato's dialogues, Plato's philosophical ideas are expressed in the form of dialectic between the main character of Socrates and interlocutors expressing various positions. In this paper I will sometimes refer to Plato and sometimes to Socrates as forwarding ideas that are found in Plato's dialogues. In this section of the paper, I would like to explore definitions of the true, the good, and beauty in Plato and Aristotle. The majority of definitions for this section of the paper come from Plato's works because, as Hans-Georg Gadamer argues in his work: The Idea of The Good in Platonic-Aristotelian Philosophy, Aristotle agrees with and develops further Plato's conception of the true, the good, and the beautiful. Therefore, where Aristotle adds to, clarifies, and develops ideas that are originally found within Plato's dialogues, I will quote Aristotle.

Truth for Plato is what accords with reality, and so Socrates says that "he who says that which is, says the truth".[6][7] The highest truth is what accords with highest reality and is most accurate, as Socrates notes: "How ridiculous that we should not think the highest truths worthy of attaining the highest accuracy".[8] The highest reality for Plato is that of the ideas or forms (I will use these terms interchangeably), particularly the highest form, which is that of

---

6   All references to Plato and Aristotle are from the *Britannica Great Books of the Western World*, Volumes 7-9. (Chicago: University of Chicago; 1952).
7   Plato, *Euthydemas*. Vol 7, p. 72a.
8   Plato, *Republic* VI. Vol 7, p. 384b.

the good. In *Republic* VI, Plato makes the distinction between appearance and reality in his Allegory of the Sun, in which Socrates likens the sun to the child of the good. The sun is that by which we see the visible world, the world of appearances. The good, like the sun, sheds light on reality. Yet we see this reality not by sight but by reason. Plato divides the world into visible and intelligible, then speaks of increasing degrees of truth that the mind may attain through four different faculties of the soul. The faculty of sense perception allows us to see the visible world, which is the lesser of what is clear and true. The faculty of conviction rises to a higher level of truth than sensory perception. Science and mathematics elevate the soul to understanding, a higher level of truth yet. And finally, reason leads to the contemplation of the ideas, which are the highest kinds of truth/realities. Our senses give us truths of the physical world, whereas reason, through contemplation of the forms, which are most real, gets us to the highest level of truths, which are purely intelligible and unknown through the senses. In dividing the world between the visible and the intelligible, Socrates says that: "Both the sections of this division have different degrees of truth, and that the copy is to the original as the sphere of opinion is to the sphere of knowledge…".[9] In this quote "copy" and "original" are in the realm of being/reality, whereas "opinion" and "knowledge" are epistemological categories. The sensory world is a copy of the original forms. Opinion has less truth than does knowledge. In addition, knowing is of being (reality), and knowing involves having true ideas (reality in my mind).

The highest idea to be known is the good. Socrates says that: "The idea of good is the highest knowledge, and that all other things become useful and advantageous only by their use of this … and without which, any other knowledge or possessions of any kind will profit us nothing".[10] The good for both Plato and Aristotle is the end in itself. Socrates tells us that the good is that "which every soul of man pursues and makes the end of all his actions, hav-

---

9 Ibid., p. 387a.
10 Plato, *Republic* VI, p. 384b-c.

ing a presentment that there is such an end...".[11] Aristotle begins his Nichomachean Ethics with: "Every art and every inquiry, and similarly every action and pursuit, is thought to aim at some good; and for this reason the good has rightly been declared to be that at which all things aim".[12] He goes on to say that:

> There is some end of the things we do, which we desire for its own sake (everything else being desired for the sake of this), and if we do not choose everything for the sake of something else ... clearly this must be the good and the chief good. Will not knowledge of it, then, have a great influence on life?[13]

The good is what we seek as an end in itself, for its own sake, and not for the sake of anything else. Knowledge of the good, as the highest end to pursue would lead to knowledge of the highest reality, or highest being. In speaking of the good as the end in itself, one must ask how this end is obtained, or what are the means to the good? In both Plato and Aristotle, the virtues of wisdom, temperance, courage and justice are often spoken of as moral virtues by which the good is achieved.

The classical virtues are depicted in Plato's *Phaedrus* in the Allegory of the Chariot. A human being has the faculties of spirit, appetite, and reason. Plato has us envision the human soul as a chariot driver who is managing two horses that are pulling us along the heavens. One horse, the spirited one, is noble, carrying the chariot driver to his ultimate heavenly destination. The other horse represents the appetites and is ignoble, pulling the chariot driver in the opposite direction and down to earth where the soul is ultimately united with a physical body. The chariot driver represents reason, which was originally directed towards the forms, but now has been pulled away by his appetites and passions (the unruly horse). The virtues are the means by which man may habituate himself towards

---

11   Ibid, p. 384d.
12   Aristotle, *Nichomachean Ethics*, GBWW Vol. 9, p. 339a.
13   Ibid, p. 339b.

the good, the true source of life, and away from the appetites and passions that are enticed by the physical world. Courage is the virtue whereby man can take action in the face of danger and avoid the temptation to pursue power as an end in itself. Temperance is the virtue whereby man can pursue moderation in the exercise of his appetites and avoid pleasure as an end in itself. Wisdom is the virtue of reason in pursuit of the good, and in applying the most appropriate application of means for the purpose of achieving the end in itself. Lastly, justice is the virtue that brings harmony and balance to the whole soul of man. This harmony of the virtues of the soul is the source of beauty in the soul.[14]

In the midst of the story about the chariot driver and the two horses, Socrates explains the soul's flight to the beautiful itself, or the beatific vision, its fall to the earth, and the theory of recollection. Socrates, in this myth, explains that:

> There was a time when with the rest of the happy band they saw beauty shining in brightness, - we philosophers following in the train of Zeus, others in company with other gods; and then we beheld the beatific vision and were initiated into a mystery which may be truly called most blessed, celebrated by us in our state of innocence, before we had any experience of evils to come, when we were admitted to the sight of apparitions innocent and simple and calm and happy, which we beheld shining in pure light, pure ourselves and not yet enshrined in that living tomb which we carry about, now that we are imprisoned in the body, like an oyster in his shell.[15]

This quote is significant for understanding the relationship between the form of the beautiful and beautiful things in the world of appearances in which we now live. In its failure to behold the truth, the soul falls to the physical world (driven by the unruly

---

14   Plato, *Phaedrus*, p. 124b-129d.
15   Plato, *Phaedrus*, p. 128c.

horse), where it is now imprisoned in a body. There are different levels of souls, based upon the degree of truth which they beheld in the previous life. Socrates explains that "the soul which has seen most of truth shall come to the birth as a philosopher, or artist, or some musical and loving nature".[16] The soul of the philosopher, because it has seen more of truth, and has had a vision of beauty, will be better able to recognize truth and beauty in the world of appearances. When the philosopher sees the beauty of an earthly lover, he is reminded of the form of the beautiful, upon which he has previously gazed. The larger context of the Phaedrus is the art of love (*eros*). Socrates speaks of eros as a kind of madness that possesses the philosopher, "which is imputed to him who, when he sees the beauty of earth, is transported with the recollection of the true beauty; he would fly away, but he cannot; he is like a bird fluttering and looking upward and careless of the world below; and he is therefore thought to be mad".[17] The beauty of earthly things and beautiful people partake in beauty itself, which the soul knew and loved before this life, and so "he who loves the beautiful is called a lover because he partakes of it".[18] The beautiful person or thing partakes of the beautiful itself, and the lover of beauty partakes of beauty itself through the beautiful person or thing. In this way, earthly beauty is a medium between the lover of the beautiful and the form of beauty itself. Beauty inspires the devotion of the lover, "whom he beholds in company with Modesty like an image placed upon a holy pedestal. He sees her, but he is afraid and falls backwards in adoration…".[19] There is a holiness connected to beauty. What is beautiful is the object of devotion. It is pure, related to modesty, and is other, set apart from the rest of reality. Yet, what is beauty?

In order to begin to understand beauty in Plato's conception of reality, I will refer to his Allegory of the Cave in *Republic* VII. Pla-

---

16   Ibid, p. 125c-d.
17   Ibid, p. 126b.
18   Plato, *Phaedrus*, p. 126b
19   Ibid, p. 128b-c

to's myth about the soul's ascent to the good has us imagine a scenario in which there is a cave with people chained facing the wall of the cave, upon which are cast shadows, which these people take to be reality, producing something like a show on the wall of the cave. These prisoners hear sounds, and see sights that are produced by others, but they take these images and sounds to be real. They then go on to form judgments and make predictions about the appearances they have observed since youth. One of these prisoners is forced from the cave to the light of day, has to reorient not only his eyesight, being forced into daylight and temporarily blinded, but he has to rethink his entire view of reality. What he thought was true was a mistake. As his eyes adjust, he is able to see the "real" world. He can see the source of the shadows, which he previously took to be reality, and he can see things like trees, birds, and heavenly bodies. Eventually, he can look at the sun, the source of all life. He has grasped the truth of the source of all being. In due time, he goes back into the cave, out of compassion for his fellow man, undergoing the painful blinding transition back into the darkness. Yet, he is ultimately rejected by his fellow humans who think he has ruined his eyesight and brought back dangerous teachings.[20]

The Allegory of the Cave is a familiar story, and its interpretation is equally familiar. But the Allegory is also related to a discussion of beauty and may be the central Platonic myth by which we understand beauty and its relation to the true and the good. The cave represents the physical world in which we human beings find ourselves. We are the prisoners, and we are held captive to the false images by means of our senses. What comes to us through sensory perception we take to be reality, but in fact, sensory perceptions give us images, opinion, often false judgment, even ignorance. We are taking copies for reality when we think we know by means of the senses. We are chasing shadows on the cave wall. In the Republic, Plato talks about not allowing the artists and their works within the ideal city because he says that art is an imitation of the shadow world (which dimly reflects the "real"), therefore art is a

---

20 Plato, *Republic* VII, p. 388a-390a

copy of a copy of beauty (assuming the art is in fact beautiful). Art is a double deception. But maybe Plato is not being serious in his discussion of the role of art in the ideal polis in the Republic? He seems to say otherwise in other dialogues, as we soon shall see.

Returning to the interpretation of the Cave: The one who leaves the cave and looks upon reality, represented by trees, birds, and heavenly bodies, is the one who transcends the realm of appearances by means of reason to contemplate reality - the forms. The sun, which represents the source of all light and life, represents the beatific vision, or the form of all forms, the good itself. All the other forms, in so far as they are ideals, partake of the form of the good. The form of beauty partakes in the good as well. Plato says that:

> In the world of knowledge the idea of good appears last of all, and is seen only with an effort; and, when seen, is also inferred to be the universal author of all things beautiful and right, parent of light and of the lord of light in this visible world, and the immediate source of reason and truth in the intellectual; and that this is the power upon which he who would act rationally either in public or private life must have his eye fixed.[21]

In the difficult ascent of the soul from opinion and appearances to knowledge and truth, the good is the highest ideal to grasp and requires the most effort. It seems that the philosopher is best prepared to make the ascent. Yet, when understood, the good is the universal author of all things, or the metaphysical ground of beauty and all things right (ethics). The good is that by which we see, and the light of the good is in human beings as reason, the power by which men act rationally in public and private life. Reason is the source of right action. In this allegory we see Plato's epistemology - knowledge is of true being, not mere sensory impressions and opinion. True being gets its reality from the good. As highest reality, the good is the source of beauty itself, and the reflection of

---

21 Plato, *Republic* VII, p. 389b-c.

beautiful things in the world. It would seem, then, that a good artist is one who contemplates the good and does his best to reflect the good through his representation in the arts. Good art is that which most accurately and excellently reflects the truth of being and of the good. I would like to think that Plato would consider a good artist to be one who depicts reality with excellence.

What is the excellence with which the artist represents reality? He must grasp the essence of beauty and accurately represent beautiful things so as to draw our mind to the form of the beautiful. The artist is a mediator between the form of beauty and sensory perceptions. The artist is the mediator of beauty and the good. What is it that the artist mediates? It is the same thing that a beautiful and virtuous, or excellent soul, mediates. The beautiful work of art and the beautiful soul exhibit harmony, symmetry, excellence, balance, purity and ultimately something of the "divine" and transcendent being.

The Good and Beauty

Aristotle, in the Nichomachean Ethics, speaks about the good as the end in itself. The good is sought for its own sake, and not for the sake of anything else. He says:

> Since there are evidently more than one end, and we choose some of these (e.g. wealth, flutes, and in general instruments) for the sake of something else, clearly not all ends are final ends; but the chief good is evidently something final. Therefore, if there is only one final end, this will be what we are seeking, and if there are more than one, the most final of these will be what we are seeking … and therefore we call final without qualification that which is always desirable in itself and never for the sake of something else.[22]

---

22   Aristotle, *Nichomachean Ethics*, p. 342c-d.

In addition, he speaks about the good as that which is according to the nature of a being. Human nature differs from animals in that we are rational beings. To be more specific, we are rational political animals. As rational beings, it is good for humans to act according to their rational nature. Aristotle says that the good for humans is the "activity of the soul which follows or implies a rational principle...".[23] Good for human beings is the use of reason to the fullest. Reason, when used fully, brings us to the knowledge of the nature of ultimate reality (truth). Hans-Georg Gadamer notes that: "...In the end it becomes fully clear that only looking to what is good ..., or to what is better or best, respectively, promises [us] real knowledge, or as we would say, "understanding" - understanding, namely, of the universe as well as the polis and the psyche".[24] The good unites our knowledge of the universe, our place in it as social beings, and knowledge of our self/ soul. Gadamer shows the agreement between Plato and Aristotle on this point about the good being knowledge of ultimate reality, using Socrates in Plato's Apology as an example of a person who lived according to reason in pursuit of the good:

> Here Socrates becomes a mythical figure in whom knowledge of the good ultimately coalesces with knowledge of the true and knowledge of being in a highest theoria as it were. Our task originates here: it is to raise this mythical unity of knowledge of the good, the true, and the real to the level of conceptual thinking, and in so doing, to make comprehensible what Aristotle shares with Plato even when he critically separates himself from him.[25]

Whatever their metaphysical differences, both Plato and Aristotle agree on the unity of the true, the good, and the beautiful, and that the good is knowledge of what is highest. If the good is knowing what is most true about reality, failure to know the nature

---

23   Aristotle, *Nichomachean Ethics*, p. 343b.
24   Gadamer, p. 26.
25   Ibid, p. 31.

of ultimate reality would be ignorance,[26] and Plato considers ignorance the source of evil for human beings.

If humans know the good, they will do the good. Socrates argues that no one knowingly does evil, since evil is to harm oneself. No one knowingly harms oneself. If we do not seek the true good it is because we are mistaken about the good; we are in ignorance about the good. We seek what we think is good, but we are in error about what is truly good for us. We may take pleasure to be the good, or we may think the good to be a duty according to custom, but these are not ultimate aims, according to Socrates.

How does one seek the good, or pursue knowledge of ultimate reality? If the good is the end in itself, then the moral virtues are a means to pursuing the good. The classical virtues, which I mentioned earlier, include courage, temperance, wisdom, and justice. The Nichomachean Ethics speaks of other classifications of virtues such as natural virtues (e.g. health, physical strength) and instrumental virtues (e.g. money, possessions). What all the virtues have in common is that they are a means to the good and are not pursued as ends in themselves. We also need to love the good in order to pursue the good. More will be said about love and the good shortly.

Seeking the good, by means of the virtues, results in a life well-lived, a happy and full life, or what some have called a life of flourishing. These descriptors of the good seem to indicate that possession of the good leads to happiness that lasts. The life lived in pursuit of the good by means of the moral virtues is a harmonious life. Harmony is one of the essential features of beauty for both Plato and Aristotle. Having examined the nature of the good, I hope next to explore some key passages from Plato's dialogues to develop a sense of how he defines beauty. Aristotle seems to agree with Plato's conception of beauty; thus, I will focus primarily on Plato's Dialogues for this section of the paper. After an analysis of beauty in Plato, I would like to make a more explicit connection

---

26   Ibid, p. 23.

between the good and beauty in order to show that beauty is a dimension of ethics.

In contemplating the meaning of words, in Plato's dialogue, *Cratylus*, Socrates and Hermogenes discuss the word *kalon* (beautiful). Socrates observes that *kalon* denotes "mind", probably related to the mind of gods and/or of men. Then he asks:

> Is not mind the beautiful? ... And are not the works of intelligence and mind worthy of praise ... And the principle of beauty does the works of beauty? ... And that principle we affirm to be mind? ... Then mind is rightly called beauty because she does the works which we recognize and speak of as the beautiful.[27]

I think we can infer from this passage that what is beautiful is a result of the work of intelligence. The works of intelligence are worthy of praise. We usually praise that which we deem good, noble and excellent. The works of the highest mind is most worthy of praise, is most excellent, and is the source of all beauty.

We see the theme of excellence inspiring praise and devotion in a passage from the *Phaedrus* from the Allegory of the Chariot: "And now they are at the spot and behold the flashing beauty of the beloved; which when the charioteer sees, his memory is carried to the true beauty, whom he beholds in company with Modesty like an image placed upon a holy pedestal."[28] Beauty is in the company of Modesty. Modesty is the virtue that is concerned with purity. In addition, beauty is "placed upon a holy pedestal". She is holy, set apart for worship. We also see the beginning of the theme of beauty as something that "flashes" or "shines forth". This shining forth has the element of excellence or glory that inspires awe. Beauty is awesome.

The *Symposium* draws our attention to the transcendental aspect of beauty. Socrates tells us that a lover of forms will begin

---

27   Plato, *Cratylus*, p. 101d-102a.
28   Plato, *Phaedrus*, p. 128c.

to reflect upon beautiful forms and begin to see what is common among them, he will see that which makes each thing beautiful. He will come to see that the beauty of the mind is greater than the outward forms of beauty. The virtuous soul, contemplating further will come to recognize the beauty of "institutions and laws", "the sciences", and from there "he will create many fair and noble thoughts and notions in boundless love of wisdom; until on that shore he grows and waxes strong, and at last the vision is revealed to him of a single science, which is the science of beauty everywhere".[29] The virtuous soul ascends from beautiful forms, to the beauty of mind, then of institutions and the sciences, until it sees what is common among all beautiful things. This "single science" I take to be the essence of beauty. Yet, in the soul's ascent in understanding beauty, the essence of beauty is not the final resting place. We are told that:

> He who has been instructed thus far in the things of love, and who has learned to see the beautiful in due order and succession, when he comes toward the end will suddenly perceive a nature of wondrous beauty ... a nature which in the first place is everlasting; not growing and decaying, or waxing and waning ... but beauty absolute, separate, simple, and everlasting, which without diminution and without increase, or any change, is imparted to the ever-growing and perishing beauties of all other things.[30]

The "nature of wondrous beauty" I take to be the transcendental form of beauty itself. Again, in this grappling with defining beauty, we see that the virtuous soul has to ascend through various, and probably difficult, stages to finally arrive at beauty itself. Again, the virtuous soul is driven to the form of beauty through love. He who through love follows the beautiful in ascending order from forms, to universal, to absolute beauty:

---

29   Plato, *Symposium*, p. 167a-d.
30   Ibid, p. 167b-c.

> At least knows what the essence of beauty is ... this is that life above all others which man should live, in the contemplation of beauty absolute ... in that communion only, beholding beauty with the eye of the mind, he will be enabled to bring forth, not images of beauty, but realities ... and bringing forth and nourishing true virtue to become the friend of God and be immortal, if mortal man may.[31]

In contemplating beauty itself, the virtuous soul is nourished in reality, and becomes a beautiful soul that is in communion with the highest being as a friend. Friendship, according to Aristotle, consists in the unity of souls. Here the virtuous soul is united with the divine. The mind, contemplating beauty in itself, is akin to knowing the mind of God.

Descending from these lofty heights of transcendent beauty, we learn in the *Phaedo* that it is the participation in this absolute beauty that makes beautiful things in the visible realm beautiful. Socrates says that: "if there be anything beautiful other than absolute beauty should there be such, that it can be beautiful only in so far as it partakes of absolute beauty ...".[32] Again, he says that he is "assured in [his] own mind that nothing makes a thing beautiful but the presence and participation of beauty in whatever way or manner obtained; for as to the manner I am uncertain, but I stoutly contend that by beauty all beautiful things become beautiful".[33] The excellence of transcendent beauty shines forth in the beautiful figures, minds, institutions, and whatever else is beautiful within the realm of our experiences.

Plato's *Republic* is where his views on beauty are most elaborated in the analogy of light, the line, and in the Allegory of the Cave, all from Book VI. Since I have spoken at length about the Allegory of the Cave, and the difference between the world of sensory perception and opinion, and that of reason and knowledge

---

31　Plato, *Symposium*, p. 167c.
32　Plato, *Phaedo*, p. 242d.
33　Ibid, p. 242d-243a.

contemplating the forms, I will focus on Socrates' discussion of beauty in *Republic* V, in which Socrates distinguishes between the philosopher who pursues knowledge, corresponding with being, and those who are content with opinion. He says:

> This is the distinction which I draw between the sight-loving, art-loving, practical class and those of whom I am speaking, and who are alone worthy of the name philosophers ... The lovers of sounds and sights ... are fond of fine tones and colors and forms and all the artificial products that are made of them, but their mind is incapable of seeing or loving absolute beauty.[34]

He who stops at sounds, colors, forms, and likenesses of the beautiful is really ignorant of true beauty, and of reality itself. He is capable of exercising opinion, which may be false, but he is incapable of having knowledge (which requires truth). We have hints of the Cave in the contrast between appearance and reality in that our senses can only get us to the judgment of opinion, whereas reason gets us to reality and knowledge. From this quote we also learn that some persons are content with "fine tones", "colors", and "all the artificial products" made from them. Yet, these minds are incapable of seeing beauty itself. There is a hint of a critique of the consumption of goods that appear beautiful and are merely pleasing to the senses without giving further thought to what makes these things beautiful. Being mindful of the source of beauty is key to true appreciation of beauty in the world of appearance.

We see the relationship between absolute and relative beauty in Plato's *Philebus*. In addition to showing how beautiful things are relative to true beauty in the absolute, we are told about the true pleasures associated with appreciating absolute beauty. These pleasures are not critiqued in the same way as we saw in Republic V. It may be because there beautiful things were being consumed, and in Philebus, beautiful things are being understood. We are told

---

34   Plato, *Republic*, p. 371a.

that: "True pleasures are those which are given by beauty of color and form, and most of those arise from smells; those of sound …".[35] And further: "When sounds are smooth and clear, and have a single pure tone, then I mean to say that they are not relatively but absolutely beautiful, and have natural pleasures associated with them."[36] Beauty produces pleasures associated with experiencing purity. Here we have a return to the theme of the beauty of purity, only this time we see purity in the visible realm in the objects of sensory perception. Again, we see the beauty of the sensory world: "measure and symmetry are beauty and virtue all the world over".[37] It is universally accepted that beauty involves measure and symmetry and perfection. We may infer from the discussions of beauty in Philebus that pleasure of the mind, contemplating beauty, is much more to be desired than the pleasure of sight, observing shadows of the beautiful.

Beauty as a kind of perfection becomes the standard[38] for the arts and has the power to transform a person's soul as a kind of moral standard. In *Republic* III Plato speaks about the influence of the arts on the soul of the youth. The arts, according to Plato, have the power to produce moral deformity or a beautiful soul, depending on how badly, or how well a work of art reflects reality. Plato thus says:

> Let our artists rather be those who are gifted to discern the true nature of the beautiful and the graceful; then will our youth dwell in a land of health, amid fair sights and sounds, and receive the good in everything; and beauty, the effluence of fair works, shall flow into the eye and ear, like a health-giving breeze from a purer region, and insensibly draw the

---

35   Plato, *Philebus*, p. 630d.
36   Ibid, p. 631d.
37   Ibid, p. 638c.
38   Plato, *Gorgias*, p. 266d.

THE BEAUTIFUL AS A
DIMENSION OF ETHICS

soul from earliest years into likeness and sympathy with the beauty of reason.[39]

It almost seems that Plato has in mind that the artist will contribute to the youth becoming a lover of wisdom by means of artistic expression carried out with excellence. This quote also supports the claim that I made earlier that the artist is a mediator of reality. They draw the soul to the true source of beauty by means of sensible signs. Art is a mediation between sensation and pure contemplation. Plato tells us that "...when a beautiful soul harmonizes with a beautiful form, and the two are cast in one mould, that would be the fairest sight to him who has eye to see it...".[40] The artist has the opportunity to both be involved with the physical beauty of youth, in addition to the formation of a beautiful soul, which soul would not only see the reality of beauty, but would be a reflection of beauty through his very being. The artist mediates beauty through his artistic representations, and in the education of the youth in the arts he helps to form a beautiful soul, which in turn reflects beauty in itself. The artist is not only creating artifacts representing beauty, but he a part of the creation of beautiful souls. The aspect of the work of the artist in the creation of beautiful souls is a function that seems to be wholly absent in Modern theories of art. Fine art is reduced to aesthetic appreciation and refining of taste.

There is another sense in which beauty is a standard. The *Timaeus* describes the beautiful as fair, proportionate, symmetrical, pleasing and balanced.[41] In the *Sophist*, we learn that discord and ugliness are due to ignorance, a disease of the soul. Discord (vs. harmony, one of the key standards of beauty), deformity, dissolution of unity, want of symmetry, lack of virtue, stupidity, lack of knowledge, and practicing sophistry are all opposites of beauty. Furthermore, "we are to regard an unintelligent soul as deformed and devoid of symmetry".[42] Not only is beauty equated with har-

---

39   Plato, *Republic* III, p. 333b-d.
40   Plato, *Republic* III, p. 333d.
41   Plato, *Timaeus*, p. 474d-475b.
42   Plato, *Sophist*, p. 557d.

mony, and symmetry, but beauty is found in the mean, in the observance of measure. Plato tells us in the Statesman that: "...For all these arts are on the watch against excess and defect, not as unrealities, but as real evils, which occasion a difficulty in action, and the excellence of beauty of every work of art is due to this observance of measure".[43] Beauty is an objective standard, according to Plato, and beauty is the same for all people. The beauty of art is the pursuit of excellence for the pleasure of the soul, as is seen from this quote from the *Laws* II"

> Are beautiful things not the same to us all, or are they the same in themselves, but not in our opinion of them? For no one will admit that forms of vice in the dance are more beautiful than forms of virtue, or that he himself delights in the forms of vice, and others in a muse of another character. And most persons say that the excellence of music is to give pleasure to our souls.[44]

To sum up: Beauty is a standard of excellence for the arts and is reflected in work that is harmonious, symmetrical, measured, pure and aims towards virtue and is pleasing to the soul.

Prior to leaving our discussion of beauty as a standard for the execution of the arts, Plato has some advice for the would-be art critic that is helpful in light of Tolstoy's discussion at the beginning of the paper about divorcing the beautiful from the good. Beauty is also an objective standard for the art critic. Plato asks:

> May we not say that in everything imitated, whither in drawing, music, or any other art, he who is to be a competent judge must possess three things; - he must know; in the first place, of what the imitation is; secondly, he must know that it is true; and thirdly, that it has been well executed in words and melodies and rhythms?.[45]

---

43 Plato, *Statesman*, p. 594c.
44 Plato, *Laws* II, p. 654a-c.
45 Plato, *Laws* II, p. 661a.

The judge of good art must possess knowledge about reality and imitation of reality, he must know whether this particular imitation of reality is accurate (true), and he must be able to judge whether this particular imitation displays excellence in execution. It sounds like the art critic must be well versed in philosophy - knowing the true, the good and the beautiful. I will end with a quote that I found interesting in light of this exploration of beauty and the standards by which to judge art. Plato says that: "music is more celebrated than any other kind of imitation, and therefore requires the greatest care of them all."[46] Music is the most appreciated of the arts and has a direct line to the soul. As such, it ought to be most excellent in its use of harmony, measuredness, and unity in the communication of the beautiful. Music, as most celebrated, is most likely to impact the souls of the youth for good or for ill.

Thus far, we have explored the good, and we have explored beauty in the works of Plato. How are the good and the beautiful related? Beauty, like the good, is sought as an end in itself. Plato argues that beauty is not a thing of utility, nor of mere pleasure. Beauty is pleasurable in so far as it partakes in the good. But we do not seek the good or beauty as a means to pleasure, then it would not be an end in itself. We seek the good because we love the good with an *eros* love. Gadamer describes this *eros* by saying that it: "... Singles out beauty as the only idea that preserves something of the former lustrousness of an idea even after our plunge into this earthly world. Beauty lights up here in our world. It shines forth most of all, and it, most of all, stimulates love in us ... Thus it awakens in the lover the longing passion for what is higher."[47] Beauty shines forth with a kind of unity and purity that is ultimately attractive, leading us from the beauty in the world to the ultimate source of all beauty. The unity resulting from participation in the Good is the primary source of beauty. Gadamer continues: "Beauty is singled out [as an object of *eros*] because it "shines forth." For after all, that means that beauty is in the realm of the visible. Actually, the

---

46 Ibid, p. 661b.
47 Gadamer, p.116.

beautiful, as the thing which is loved, is surpassingly "pure" beauty. It stands fully visible in its lustrousness."[48] Beauty, in connection with purity and unity is glorious and inspires devotion within the visible world.

The Beautiful as an Ethical Category

The beauty of art, exhibiting symmetry, unity, harmony and balance in the forms of artistic expression, are for Plato, reflections of the beauty that is in the sensible order, which in turn reflects the reality of the forms, especially that of the form of Beauty itself. Beauty in art, then can only be present when those creating art, and those appreciating art are in tune with reality and the end in itself. One must know the good and the means to the good in order to recognize the many faceted reflections of beauty in the world of appearances. In knowing the good, one has rational justification for the good. Ethics is that area of philosophy that is particularly concerned with giving rational justification for the answer to the question "what is the good?" Rational justification is given by means of the dialectic. Gadamer recognizes this when he says: "Plato advances the true dialectical art of giving justification, which submits assertions about the good to question and answer".[49] Dialectic is a public means of seeking and arriving at the truth. In this case it is a public means for arriving at the truth about what is good for man as a rational being.

In arguing that Beauty is an ethical category, I will begin with examining the search for the good for the individual person. I will argue, using Soren Kierkegaard's claim, that on the individual, personal, ethical level, the purity of heart (virtue) is to will one thing - the good.[50] In addition to the life of the virtuous individual, I will suggest, referencing Plato, that the good produces beauty as the good is the source of unity in every area of life. This unity is

---

48   Ibid, p.116.
49   Gadamer, p. 41.
50   Kierkegaard, Soren. *Purity of Heart is to Will One Thing* (New York: Harper Torchbooks; 1956).

beautiful in both this life and beyond. The good is the source of unity between the forms (as the highest form), between the world of sense perception and reason (we see this in the artist as mediator between the true, the good, and the beautiful), in the world of nature (science and mathematics leading us to an understanding of reality), between persons in love and in friendships (the good as the basis of friendship and love), within the polis (Plato compares the polis to a well-ordered soul), and finally, beauty is a means for uniting the soul with the form of the good, the highest reality, in the beatific vision.

Soren Kierkegaard, in his *Purity of Heart is to Will One Thing*, focuses on the moral responsibility of the lone individual. He argues that the purity of heart is to will one thing, that one thing being the good. We saw in Plato's definition of beauty, that one of the essential features of beauty was purity. Purity has the element of not being mixed, of being one, of having unity, or harmony. The ethical dimension of beauty for the individual is purity of heart. The pure heart will singlemindedly pursue the good. Purity of heart is a virtuous soul, and as we saw with Aristotle, virtue is a means to the good. Virtue is what brings about the harmony of the soul. A harmonious soul, for both Plato and Aristotle is what makes for a good person. A good person reflects reality and the good and is thus a beautiful person.

In contrast with the pure of heart is the double minded: "The person who wills one thing that is not the Good, he does not truly will one thing. It is a delusion, and illusion, a deception, a self-deception that he wills only one thing. For in his innermost being he is, he is bound to be, double-minded".[51] The opposite of purity of heart is double mindedness. Again, Kierkegaard observes: "In truth to will one thing, then, can only mean to will the Good, because every other object is not a unity; and the will that only wills that object, therefore, must become double-minded".[52] If purity of heart is to seek the good single mindedly, then Kierkegaard asks of

---

51 Kierkegaard, p.55.
52 Ibid, p.66.

double mindedness: "Is not this evil, like evil persons, in disagreement with itself, divided against itself?"[53] The double minded is a house divided, a person whose soul lacks unity and harmony. A divided soul is inharmonious, lacking unity, ugly and morally evil. Yet, the soul that with single mind pursues the good, finds what ultimately satisfies, is at one with itself, and with all those who through all ages also seek the good.

The good, as one, for the pure heart as the individual who is single mindedly seeking the good, is what unites an individual with all other individuals. Kierkegaard asks: "And what is your attitude towards others? Are you at one with all - by willing one thing? Or do you contentiously belong to a party, or is your hand raised against every man and every man's hand raised against you? Do you wish for all others what you wish for yourself?".[54] We can infer from this quote that the individual, seeking the good for himself, will in brotherly love, want to seek the good for his fellow man. The good then is the source of true human community. It is the basis of the moral law, connected with human nature as an end in itself. Kierkegaard goes on to ask:

> Do you do unto others what you will that they should do unto you - by willing only one thing? For this will is the eternal order that governs all things, that brings you into union with the dead, and with the men whom you never see, with foreign people whose language and customs you do not know, with all men upon the whole earth, who are related to eachother by blood and eternally related to the Divine by eternity's task of willing only one thing.[55]

The good as the source of unity among people is also the source of unity between humans and the Divine, according to Kierkegaard. We are "related to the Divine" by a task given by the Divine to will only one thing. It is the goal, not only of individual human

---

53   Ibid, p.66.
54   Kierkegaard, p. 205.
55   Ibid, p. 205-206.

THE BEAUTIFUL AS A
DIMENSION OF ETHICS

beings to seek the good with single minded focus, but it is also the task of humanity as a whole to pursue the good. This is because we are made to seek the good. It is the chief end of man to pursue the good.

What results from individuals, and whole communities of men, who single mindedly pursue the good? The beauty of unity and holiness is the result of single-minded pursuit of the good. This beauty begins in the unity of a well-ordered soul. It radiates outwards in the harmony between body and soul in the beautiful person - beautiful inwardly and in form. The harmony of individuals in pursuit of the good leads to a well-ordered polis, as Plato describes in the *Republic* when he compares the well-ordered soul to the well-ordered human society. In this well-ordered society, where the good is pursued, the arts (*techne*) are a means to the true, and the beautiful. In the realm of aesthetics, art is an imitation of nature and serves to unite man with his world.

John Dewey, in his *Art as Experience*, recognizes the Greek unity between cosmos and polis when he observes that the ancients saw art as integral to daily life, and then he draws a contrast to Modern conceptions of the role of art. Dewey says that:

> Painting and sculpture were organically one with architecture, as that was one with the social purpose that buildings served. Music and song were intimate parts of the rites and ceremonies in which the meaning of group life was consummated ... Under such conditions, it is not surprising that the Athenian Greeks, when they came to reflect upon art, formed the idea that it is an act of reproduction, or imitation ... music was an integral part of the ethos and the institutions of the community. The idea "art for art's sake" would not have been even understood ... There must then be historic

reasons for the rise of the compartmental conception of fine art.[56]

Dewey's observation draws us to the unity within Plato's Athens, a unity that is reflected in art and culture, but it also draws attention to the fact that we do not now live in that world, if in fact it ever existed. We have lost the unity between the good and the beautiful that attaches to art as imitation of nature. We now study "fine art" as if it were an extinct species, reflecting a dissociation from the good as transcendent referent. Yet, before leaving Dewey, it is important to note that even though he is a theorist living in the world of disenchantment, he recognizes that the artist is in touch with and produces something good. He says:

> The process of art in production is related to the esthetic in perception organically - as the Lord God in creation surveyed His work and found it good. Until the artist is satisfied in perception with what he is doing, he continues shaping and reshaping. The making comes to an end when its result is experienced as good - and that experience comes out not by mere intellectual and outside judgement but in direct perception. An artist, in comparison with his fellows, is one who is not only especially gifted in powers of execution but in unusual sensitivity to the qualities of things.[57]

The artist is the producer and judge of what is good. He is a kind of perfectionist who has unique gifts for producing excellence. And in this excellence, there is beauty. But this goodness and beauty, for Dewey, and the rest of us who inhabit the disenchanted world of Plato's Cave has no outside referent to the Beautiful. The artist and the art critic become the determiners of beauty in a time of disenchantment. Without the Good, as an ultimate standard for both ethics and beauty, we are left with subjective standards for

---

56 Dewey, John. *Art as Experience* (New York: The Berkley Publishing Group; 1934), p. 6.
57 Dewey, p. 51.

the good and the beautiful. The loss of unity in community within the *polis*, and between persons, may be traced back to the loss of unity within the self, and our not being true to the single purpose of pursuit of the good.

V. Conclusion

Before concluding, I would like to make some suggestions about the Platonic-Aristotelian contribution to disenchantment, and to what that view contributes to the place we are now - studying "fine art" in the abstract rather than in a context of integrated community. In this discussion I will relate Taylor's disenchantment to Plato's Cave. In my mind they are both references to the immanent world, a world that is known primarily through sensory perception. It is a view of the world that limits knowledge to empirical data. The road to disenchantment begins with unresolved philosophical problems within the Platonic conception of reality. To mention a few, these problems include the epistemological difficulty there is in ascending from life in the cave, and relying on sensory perception, to using reason to know the forms. This difficulty of knowing what is most important and highest means that what humans need most, the good, is not clear and not easily knowable. When the soul does make the difficult ascent to the form of the good, to the beatific vision, this "vision" is non-cognitive and may only be related by means of allegory and analogy. The use of reason seems to be lauded by Plato, but then bypassed when attempting to grasp highest reality by means of contemplation. Lastly, Plato's conception of the forms as eternally existing independent entities of sorts has been seen as highly problematic.

Aristotle sees difficulties with Plato's forms and thinks that they double reality. Instead, Aristotle locates the form of each thing within the thing itself, within the physical world. Yet, this move by Aristotle does not seem to get us out of the Cave in that we have lost a transcendent grounding of the true, the good, and the beautiful by losing Plato's transcendent forms. Both Plato and Aristotle's metaphysics seem inadequate to ground the true, the good, and the beautiful - leaving us within the Cave, or in the world of disenchantment.

One way around this metaphysical problem is to ground the true, the good, and the beautiful in the being of a personal, transcendent Creator, which is what Thomas Aquinas attempts to do in his synthesis of the Platonic-Aristotelian categories with the Christian worldview. The true, the good, and the beautiful are aspects of the being of God the Creator. God creates reality. Things are created with a nature. It is good for a being to act according to its nature as created by God. Beauty in the creation reflects the beauty and holiness of the Creator. Yet, some of the problems present in Plato remain for Aquinas. For example, the good/ beatific vision in Aquinas is still hard to attain by means of reason, making the good not clear to reason, thus leaving the vast numbers of humankind with an excuse for not knowing the good. The Beatific Vision in the afterlife is still non-cognitive in nature for Aquinas. If God created this world for humankind and intended the Beatific Vision for man as the ultimate goal and source of human happiness, one wonders why God did not bypass the created order and create man in unison with the Beatific Vision to begin with.

Charles Taylor's *Secular Age* implies that heaven, the Beatific Vision, and the promise of true happiness in the afterlife was an inadequate view of reality for life in the here and now. In the world of disenchantment, we discovered that all of our desires may be fully satisfied here on earth, making a transcendent referent like the forms, or God, superfluous. There is no need to go beyond the Cave, or there is no distinction between the Cave and life outside the Cave - the goal of both is individual pleasure.

The disenchantment of the world is the loss of transcendent sources of the true, the good, and the beautiful. Have the philosophers failed in their duties, according to Plato's view of the work of philosophers? If art reflects the philosophy of the day, and the philosophy of the day is purely immanent - the world of the Cave - then the problem, if there is a problem, is not with art, but with philosophy. Nietzsche said that God is dead, and we are the ones who killed him. We made God culturally irrelevant. Why have philosophers stopped doing metaphysics in pursuit of the real? Why are we all practical materialists now? I believe we are where we are in regard to truth - in the Cave - because of the prevailing skepticism of our day. Socrates fiercely fought against the skepticism of his day, in the form of Sophistry. Where is the Socrates of our day? Do the philosophers still have the duty to transcend the Cave in pursuit of the true, the good, and the beautiful by means of reason, justifying our beliefs through dialectic so as to arrive at knowledge of the highest reality?

A unity between the good and the beautiful in Plato and Aristotle is a means to understanding a standard for ethics and aesthetics. Beauty is an ethical category. If one knows the good, and pursues the virtues in light of the good, the result is harmony (an aspect of beauty) between thought and action. Knowing the good results in doing the good for the well-ordered, harmonious soul. Evil is ignorance, or the failure to know the good, and thus doing what is harmful to oneself and others in following passions or mere utility, and living less than a human existence as was evidenced by Plato's Allegory of the Cave, which life is inharmonious, disordered, ignorant, and ugly. A well-ordered and beautiful soul will know what is true, will love and pursue the good in every dimension of life, and will be a beautiful person, as well as cherish what is beautiful in all aspects of life including the arts, education, science, nature, the *polis*, and technology.

Neo-Neo-Pythagoreanism: Number as Metaphysics, Mathematics as Human Life

Jason Morgan, Ph.D.

Introduction: On the Numerification of the World

Before the rise of the modern state, individual relationships, including often the paramount individual relationship between a person and God or other supernatural force(s), were the laborious central business of daily life. The Other in all of his or her complexity was the given of human existence. The infinite diversity of Creation was the immediate fact present to the human mind.

Today, however, human life is increasingly understood and expressed in numerical terms. State control over ever-larger populations has tended to be a function of statistical averaging, of the numerical massification of individuals into political groups. Jean-Jacques Rousseau premised his "general will" on the ability of statistics and majority rule (under the Roman, not Spartan, model) to show forth the body politic.[1] Censuses, cadastral surveys, social security regimes, national tax offices, and public health programs have tended further to strip individuals of their individuality, situating human persons as numbered objects under the dominion of

---

[1] See, e.g., Paul Weirich, "Rousseau on Proportional Majority Rule," *Philosophy and Phenomenological Research*, vol. 47, no. 1 (Sept., 1986), pp. 111-126, Peter J. Steinberger, "Hobbes, Rousseau and the Modern Conception of the State," *The Journal of Politics*, vol. 70, no. 3 (Jul., 2008), pp. 595-611, Alexandra Oprea, "Pluralism and the General Will: The Roman and Spartan Models in Rousseau's *Social Contract*," *The Review of Politics*, vol. 81 (2019), pp. 573-596, and Christopher Kutz, "The Collective Work of Citizenship," *Legal Theory*, vol. 8 (2002), pp. 471-494.

a centralized power.² Jeremy Bentham's Panopticon, and Michel Foucault's meditations on the meanings and consequences of such an idea, brought to a head the crisis of legitimacy of the modern managerial state.³

The rise of Big Data and the centralization of human experience under proprietary regimes of epistemological control (known rather euphemistically as "Big Tech," but comprising much more than the software and hardware of Silicon Valley, for example the surveillance techniques of the People's Republic of China) may appear to be an extension of this trend of the numerification of human life. However, in this paper I will argue that, not only has the tendency to see human beings and human experience in numerical terms been latent in Western culture from the beginnings of recorded history, but that in recent decades this life-as-number paradigm—what I call here Pythagoreanism and neo-Pythagoreanism—has itself given way to an entirely new numerification scheme, "neo-neo-Pythagoreanism".

Neo-neo-Pythagoreanism, I argue, drawing heavily on the work of French philosopher Alain Badiou, is the transformation of not just epistemology but metaphysics into number, and vice versa. This new kind of numerification of the human person represents a radical break with Pythagoreanisms (numero-epistemological schemes) of the past, and presents serious challenges for the integrity of the human person under any modern political regime. Big Tech, and the Big Data technologies and totalizing philosophies which undergird it, means the dissolution of the human person, not back from Rousseauan mass-man to pre-modern individual, but from mass-man to post-modern non-person, from a face in a crowd to a cipher with an existence equaling, as Badiou asserts,

---

2   For one example of many, see Edward Higgs, *The Information State in England: The Central Collection of Information on Citizens since 1500* (Hampshire, England: Palgrave Macmillan, 2004).
3   Michel Foucault, *Discipline and Punish: The Birth of the Prison* (New York, NY: Random House, 1977).

zero.⁴ Neo-neo-Pythagoreanism is thus not just a political but also an existential problem for all human beings.

From One or Many to Number Itself: Pythagoreanism and Neo-Pythagoreanism in History

In Western philosophy, arguably the most persistent and intractable tension is between the One and the Many.⁵ There is obviously diversity in the world, but there is similarity, too. All the lemons on a lemon tree, all the lemon trees in a grove, all the groves in a valley, all the valleys in the world—things can be distinct but also similar, separate but also part of a group. Why? How, if at all, are the Many also One? How does the One stoop to become scattered among the Many? Plato's Forms and Aristotle's (and St. Thomas Aquinas') moderate realism—the One is in Heaven and the Many "participate" in it, or the One is in each of the Many and the mind grasps the Many as also a One—are the perennial dueling solutions to the question of universals. Things can be counted in two ways, but how to make sense of the contradictions that seem to arise from this fact?⁶

While Plato and Aristotle set the tone for most of subsequent philosophical consideration about universals, there has always been

---

4   See Byung-Chul Han, *The Expulsion of the Other* (Cambridge, England: Polity Press, 2018), pp. 74-76.
5   A good overview is Curtis L. Hancock, "The One and the Many: The Ontology of Science in Aristotle and Thomas Aquinas," *The Review of Metaphysics*, vol. 69, no. 2 (Dec., 2015), pp. 233-259, citing *inter alia* important works such as Charles Bonaventure Crowley, ed. Peter A. Redpath, *Aristotelian-Thomistic Philosophy of Measure and the International System of Units (SI)* (Lanham, MD: University Press of America, 1996), Peter A. Redpath, *A Not-So-Elementary Christian Metaphysics* (Manitou Springs, CO: Socratic Press, 2012), and Curtis L. Hancock, "The Nature of Metaphysics and Science: The Problem of the One and the Many in Thomas Aquinas," in Mark Pestana, ed., *Metaphysics* (Rijeka: InTech Publishing, 2012).
6   See, e.g., Aristotle, *Metaphysics*, Book X, Ch. 1, 1052a.15-1053b.9, in Aristotle, ed. Richard McKeon, *The Basic Works of Aristotle* (New York, NY: Random House, 1941), pp. 834-838.

a third, much more minority approach: number. The One and the Many—singularity or plurality—have long held sway over philosophical reasoning, but a few philosophers have always gone beyond these debates to posit number itself as the organizing principle of the cosmos. Number cast a spell over ancient Greek philosophy to an extent not often recognized today. Plato famously (but perhaps apocryphally) had written over the entrance to his Academy that nobody ignorant of geometry was allowed to enter.[7] Aristotle, too, was fascinated with numbers, and the ancient Greek philosophical milieu in general spent a great deal of time pondering the puzzles of numerals, counting, grouping, and the procedures and philosophical underpinnings of arithmetic.

Some, however, inverted the relationship between thought and number and made number into a kind of universal code. Some even made number into a magic force, or the ground of being, a metaphysics of integers and square roots. The most infamous Greek numero-ontologist was Pythagoras.

As with Socrates, Shakyamuni, and Confucius, Pythagoras died philosophically intestate. So, we have to rely on those who came after him for information about his life and ideas. Probably the most frequently cited source is Aristotle, who writes in his *Metaphysics* that the Pythagoreans "thought [mathematical] principles were the principles of all things. [...] Numbers seemed to be the first things in the whole of nature, they supposed the elements of numbers to be the elements of all things, and the whole heaven to be a musical scale and a number."[8] Since at least the time of this introduction in the works of Aristotle, the idea of Pythagoras as a kind of mathematical wizard or soothsayer has remained strong in the Western imagination.

---

7   David R. Lloyd, "Symmetry and Beauty in Plato," *Symmetry*, vol. 2 (2010), p. 458

8   Aristotle, *Metaphysics*, Book I, 5, 985b.23-p86a1, cited in Edward Grant, *A History of Natural Philosophy: From the Ancient World to the Nineteenth Century* (Cambridge, England: Cambridge University Press, 2007), pp. 15-16

There are many legends about Pythagoras, to be sure. It is difficult to know exactly how much of the Pythagorean imaginary is real. And, as Leonid Zhmud provocatively asked in a 1989 essay, did Pythagoras really say that "All is number?" in the first place? Zhmud, and some other philosophers, argue that Aristotle's claims about Pythagoras' beliefs have been inflated beyond what Aristotle originally intended to convey.[9] However, taken together the circumstantial and second-hand evidence seem to indicate that Pythagoras and his followers formed a religious cult of numbers, a cult also obsessed with endless other superstitions. For example, the Pythagoreans' alleged obsession with beans is well known. Indeed, some scholars have gone so far as to suggest that Pythagoras professed "reincarnationist veganism".[10] There is doubt about whether any of the legends are true, and also doubt about whether Pythagoras and his group were really as impassioned about numbers as later writers believed (or invented). But we can bracket the actual life and teachings of Pythagoras, whatever they were, and

---

9   Leonid J. Zhmud, "'All Is Number?' Basic Doctrine of Pythagoreanism Reconsidered," *Phronesis*, vol. 34 (1989), cited in Gabrielle Cornelli, "A Review of Aristotle's Claim Regarding Pythagoreans['] Fundamental Beliefs: All Is Number?" *Filosofia Unisinos: Unisinos Journal of Philosophy*, vol. 17, no. 1 (January-April, 2016). See also "b. Pythagoras and Pythagoreanism," in Patricia Curd, "New Work on the Presocratics," *Journal of the History of Philosophy*, vol. 49, no. 1 (2011), pp. 6-9. For a counter-argument to Zhmud see Owen Goldin, "The Pythagorean Table of Opposites, Symbolic Classification, and Aristotle," *Science in Context*, vol. 28, no. 2 (2015), pp. 171-193.

10   Kevin Blankinship, "Suffering the Sons of Eve: Animal Ethics in al-Maʿarrī's *Epistle of the Horse and the Mule*," *Religions*, vol. 11, 412 (2020), p. 5, citing Matthew Melvin-Koushki, "The New Brethren of Purity: Ibn Turka and the Renaissance of Neopythagoreanism in the Early Modern Persian Cosmopolis," in Robert Aurélien, Irene Caiazzo, and Constantin Macris, eds., *Companion to the Reception of Pythagoras and Pythagoreanism*, 2 vols. (Leiden: Brill, forthcoming). It should be noted that there is much lesser known "Pythagoras" whose pharmaceutical treatises were known to medieval Muslim thinkers. See Aileen R. Das, "Probable New Fragments and a Testimonium on Galen's Commentary on Plato's *Timaevs*," *The Classical Quarterly*, vol. 69, no. 1 (2019), p. 396, fn. 69.

focus on his name as shorthand for the elevation of number above all, an idea which without doubt existed in the ancient world.

In essence, Pythagoreanism, which perhaps had little to do with Pythagoras himself, was the redirection of the problem of the One and the Many into the hyper-literal realm of numerology. On the numerological scheme, counting counted for infinitely more than what was being counted. Counting, in extreme cases, became being itself. What Pythagoras (probably) thought of as the "music of the spheres," the harmonics of the planets based on number, was, for later Pythagoreans, much more important than the planets themselves. The universe was somehow a function of number or of mathematics itself. Number trumped all.

While Western philosophy is often summed up in the popular press as "footnotes to Plato," with Aristotle as yang to Plato's yin, the truth is that Pythagoreanism has always had a tertiary hold on men's minds beyond the traditional Plato-Aristotle dichotomy.[11] Or, perhaps it is more accurate to say that all of post- or even contemporary Pythagorean thought has been what later came to be known as "neo-Pythagoreanism," or the abstraction, from the legends and superstitions associated with Pythagoras, of the purer theory of the ultimate reality of numbers and math. In fact, a skimming glance through Western philosophy will reveal that, while Platonism and Aristotelianism, idealism and realism (and the nominalism or atomism associated with William of Ockham and Greek philosophers such as Leucippus and Democritus) has waxed and waned, neo-Pythagoreanism has almost always enjoyed a small but devoted coterie of enthusiasts. Western philosophy may be footnotes to Plato, but among the most consistently recurring footnotes is neo-Pythagoreanism.

For example, following the "first published account of Pythagorean teachings" by "a later disciple, Philolaus of Croton or Tarentum," neo-Pythagoreanism was an important strain of

---

11   Alfred North Whitehead, *Process and Reality* (New York, NY: MacMillan, 1978 (1929)), Part II, Discussions and Applications, Chapter I, Fact and Form, p. 39.

neo-Platonism in post-Classical Greece.¹² Neo-Pythagoreanism was popular in Rome, too: in an 1894 lecture (and subsequent 1895 essay) philosopher Franz Brentano notes that "Apollonius of Tyana and Moderatus of Gades" were neo-Pythagoreans "under Nero," while another Roman neo-Pythagorean named "Nichomachus of Gerasa lived before the time of the Antonines."¹³ The "philosopher of the Arabs" al-Kindī was a neo-Pythagorean.¹⁴ Muhammad Biruni (Abu Rayhan al-Biruni), a Muslim polymath in the late tenth and early eleventh centuries, was a Pythagorean of the first rank.¹⁵ Historian of Central Asia and the Muslim world S. Frederick Starr says of him that "More than any other thinker of the Middle Ages—East or West—Biruni embraced and acted on the maxim of Pythagoras [that] 'things are numbers'."¹⁶ Early Christian thinkers St. Augustine and Boethius are said to have been influenced by neo-Pythagoreanism in some of their theological work, while later Christians Nicholas of Cusa and Thierry of Chartres are held up as a counter-example to the "mathesis narrative: the 'neo-Kantian narrative of modernity's origins—common to Husserl, Koyré, Cassirer, and Heidegger, and centered on the

---

12   Joseph Owens, *A History of Ancient Western Philosophy* (New York, NY: Appleton-Century-Crofts, 1959), p. 33, and Therese Scarpelli and Staff, "Review of Carl A. Huffman, *Archytas of Tarentum: Pythagorean, Philosopher, and Mathematician King*, Cambridge: Cambridge University Press, 2005," *The Review of Metaphysics*, vol. 60, no. 2 (December, 2006), pp. 406-408.
13   Franz Brentano, "The Four Phases of Philosophy and Its Present Condition," *Philosophy Today*, vol. 43, no. 1 (Spring, 1999), p. 18, endnote 18
14   Taneli Kukkonen, "Review of Peter Adamson and Peter E. Portman, eds. and trs., *The Philosophical Works of al-Kindī*, Oxford-New York: Oxford University Press, 2012," *Journal of the History of Philosophy*, vol. 53, no. 3 (July, 2015), pp. 546-547
15   See, e.g., Md. Wasim Aktar and Dwaipayan Sengupta, "Fundamentals of Theoretical and Applied Mathematics: Role of Ancient Arabian and Egyptian Scientists," *International Journal of Medical and Biological Frontiers*, vol. 17, iss. 3 (2011), p. 263.
16   S. Frederick Starr, *Lost Enlightenment: Central Asia's Golden Age from the Arab Conquest to Tamerlane* (Princeton, NJ: Princeton University Press, 2013), p. 275, citing Cecil Maurice Bowra, *The Greek Experience* (Cleveland, 1957), p. 166

dramatic leap into mathematized or geometrized vision of the cosmos by Galileo and Descartes'."[17] Neo-Pythagoreanism under the guise of "harmony of the spheres" discourse influenced twelfth- to thirteenth-century mathematician Fibonacci through to nineteenth-century composers such as Claude Debussy and Frederic Chopin.[18] Renaissance philosopher Marsilio Ficino is noted for having been an enthusiastic neo-Pythagorean along "Iamblichean neo-Platonis[t]" lines.[19] Some have found neo-Pythagoreanism in the work of Isaac Newton and St. Thomas More.[20] In a 2002 essay, contemporary philosopher M.C. Bradley finds it necessary to entertain the possibility that another philosopher, Richard Swinburne, may have lapsed into "neo-Pythagoreanism" in deploying the "Bayesian version" of the "fine-tuning argument".[21] Far from

---

17   Denis Robichaud, "Review of David Albertson, *Mathematical Theologies: Nicholas of Cusa and the Legacy of Theirry of Chartres*, Oxford Studies in Historical Theology, New York, NY: Oxford University Press, 2014," *Journal of the History of Philosophy*, vol. 53, no. 2 (April, 2015), p. 333. Quotation above from Albertson book under review. See also Svetla Slaveva-Griffin, "Review of J. Kalvesmaki, *The Theology of Arithmetic: Number Symbolism in Platonism and Early Christianity* (Hellenic Studies 59), Washington, DC: Center for Hellenic Studies, 2013," *The Classical Review*, vol. 64, no. 2 (2014), pp. 429-431, Eugene TeSelle, "Review of Alastair H.B. Logan, *Gnostic Truth and Christian Heresy: A Study in the History of Gnosticism*," *Church History*, vol. 66, no. 3 (September, 1997), pp. 538-539, and Christiane L. Joost-Gaugier, *Measuring Heaven: Pythagoras and His Influence on Thought and Art in Antiquity and the Middle Ages* (Ithaca, NY: Cornell University Press, 2006).

18   Rima Povilionienè, "Musica Fibonacciana: Aesthetic and Practical Approach," *New Sound*, vol. 50, no. II (2017)

19   Christopher S. Celenza, "Pythagoras in the Renaissance: The Case of Marsilio Ficino," *Renaissance Quarterly*, vol. 52, no. 3 (Autumn, 1999), pp. 668 ff. See also Gabrielle Cornelli, "Review of Phillip Sidney Horky, *Plato and Pythagoreanism* (Oxford University Press, 2013)," *American Journal of Philology*, vol. 136 (2015), pp. 353-357.

20   Niccolò Guicciardini, "The Role of Musical Analogies in Newton's Optical and Cosmological Work," *Journal of the History of Ideas*, vol. 74, no. 1 (January, 2013), pp. 45-67, and Yelena Mazour-Matsusevitch, "(Neo)Pythagorean Vision in Thomas More's *Utopia*," *Moreana*, vol. 51, nos. 195&196 (2014), pp. 85-102

21   M.C. Bradley, "The Fine-Tuning Argument: The Bayesian Version," *Religious Studies*, vol. 38 (2002), pp. 397-398

expiring with the cult of magic beans in ancient Greece, Pythagoreanism, in the form of neo-Pythagoreanism, has enjoyed a long and illustrious life in Western thought.

Proto-Neo-Neo-Pythagoreanism: Alain Badiou and his Times

While neo-Pythagoreanism has a storied tradition as an alternative strain of Western philosophy, advances in mathematics and geometry in the seventeenth century and thereafter precipitated what might be called "neo-neo-Pythagoreanism," or new and sometimes nearly wholesale departures in numerical epistemology. To give perhaps the most salient example, the calculus invented by Isaac Newton and Gottfried Wilhelm Leibniz and the radically new geometrical insights of Bernhard Riemann were married to the disruptions in philosophical anthropology engendered by Rene Descartes (a mathematician), David Hume, Immanuel Kant, John Locke, Georg Wilhelm Friedrich Hegel, Charles Darwin, and Karl Marx to produce an inversion of the human person, a way of thinking about humanity not as created by God but as a precipitate of a universe ultimately either fully materialistic or else divided between matter and spirit. Finally, with the advance of mathematical thinking (and modern "science," which is not scientific but rather the substitution of mathematical logic for metaphysical ordering), a re-founding of philosophical anthropology as neither spirit nor matter, but as ultimately number, occurred.[22]

This process accelerated as rapid advances in mathematics and science in the late Renaissance and thereafter caused many philosophers to doubt the integration of the human person and the surrounding world. The "disenchantment of the world" which Baconian scientific inquiry (in reality anti-scientific, as Peter Redpath has pointed out—I retain the term "science" as convenient convention) tended to produce was paired with a rise in materialistic

---

22   On "science," see Robert A. Delfino, "The Cultural Dangers of Scientism and Common Sense Solutions," *Studia Gilsoniana*, vol. 3 (supplement) (2014), pp. 485-496.

thinking.[23] Increasingly, philosophers and scientists began to argue that the universe is a kind of perpetual motion machine, perhaps started by a "Supreme Being" in the distant past but now almost entirely left to run on its own accord, following the physical "laws" which Newton and others had declared sovereign over every part of creation. If this was true, then there was little need for metaphysics to explain physical phenomena. By extension, humans, too began to be seen as complicated machines. Descartes was intrigued by automatons, for example, and the later rise of psychoanalysis was predicated on the operation of the human mind according to various axioms of behavior and thought, or of the underlying structure of cognition.[24]

Unlike the Pythagoreans, who thought that "all is number," or the neo-Pythagoreans, who in one way or another thought that numerological insights would provide clues to the true nature of the cosmos or of some aspect of reality, neo-neo-Pythagoreans rely on the complete overhaul of thinking itself into a sub-species of mathematics. This neo-neo-Pythagoreanism is the prevalent mode of philosophical anthropology today, among both the vulgar and the elect.[25]

Even with the rise of neo-neo-Pythagoreanism, however, the mind presented a problem for neo-neo-Pythagoreans, dialectical materialists, and other latter-day neo-Platonists. Marx and later materialist philosophers had no satisfactory answer to the question

---

23   See Peter A. Redpath, "Why Descartes Was Not a Philosopher," in Brendan Sweetman, ed., *The Failure of Modernism: The Cartesian Legacy and Contemporary Pluralism* (Mishawaka, Indiana: American Maritain Association, 1999), pp. 10-21.

24   On Descartes, see John Sutton, "Review of Dennis Des Chene, *Spirits and Clocks: Machine and Organism in Descartes* (Ithaca and London: Cornell University Press, 2001)," *British Journal for the History of Science* (June, 2003), pp. 233-235, and Minsoo Kang, "The Mechanical Daughter of Rene Descartes: The Origin and History of an Intellectual Fable," *Modern Intellectual History*, vol. 14, no. 3 (2007), pp. 633-660.

25   See "Philosophy and Mathematics, or the Story of an Old Couple," in Alain Badiou with Gilles Haéri, tr. Susan Spitzer, *In Praise of Mathematics* (Cambridge, UK: Polity, 2016), pp. 20-45.

NEO-NEO-PYTHAGOREANISM 115

of how humans know, the problem in Marx' and the Marxists' case being greatly compounded by the denial of a non-material realm at all. For dialectical materialists, it remained, ironically, a mystery how matter could "dialogue" with even itself, producing the events of history which Hegel's grounded *Geist*, they argued, was supposed to engender. The elevation of class to a universal category in Marxism ended up investing a side-effect of mathematical ontology, a pure statement of neo-neo-Pythagoreanism, by one of the most radical Marxian thinkers, Alain Badiou.

Alain Badiou was born in Morocco and came of age in a rapidly decolonizing Greater France. The transformative month in Badiou's life was arguably May of 1968, when a shockwave of protests and street violence swept across Paris, catalyzed by Marxist fixations among the intellectual class and disaffections in trade unions throughout France. Badiou was by that time a committed Maoist, and he internalized the doctrines of Mao and the necessity, as Mao saw it, of the Communist Party to lead the masses to "liberation" from bourgeoisie enslavement and alienation. Badiou's urgent philosophical project was virtually coterminous with his political fervor.[26] His task, as he saw it, was to articulate a theory of human life, and especially of ontology, which would allow for the masses to be led by the Party, but which would also preclude the specter of Fascism. Badiou saw this political problem starkly as a problem of the Many (the masses, led by the Party) and the One (Fascism).[27] So, Badiou needed an anti-metaphysics, which would so trammel reality as to make the coalescence of masses under a charismatic leader impossible. Badiou's solution would effect the full transformation of neo-Pythagoreanism into the radically different neo-neo-Pythagoreanism which dominates the world under the guise of Big Tech and Big Data today.

---

26   On Badiou's political milieu, see, e.g., Adrian Johnston, "The Right Left: Alain Badiou and the Disruption of Political Identities," *Yale French Studies*, no. 116/117 (2009), pp. 55-78.
27   Cf. Ian Hunter, "Heideggerian Mathematics: Badiou's *Being and Event* as Spiritual Pedagogy," *Representations*, no. 134 (Spring, 2016), pp. 116-156.

In his earliest work, Badiou engaged in polemics against another French philosopher, Gilles Deleuze, whose ideas of the rhizome were an attempt to think human society in terms of anti-metaphor. The endlessly and randomly ramifying rhizome was, for Deleuze, indicative of how humans could move through time and adapt to contingency without turning to a Fascist strongman to order society from above.[28] Badiou, in turn, called this rhizomatic thinking "the fascism of the potato," sharply criticizing Deleuze for not taking seriously Mao's dictum that "'the One has no existence as entity,' since for the Maoist 'there is only unity from movement, all is process".[29] "'Only a moron (*seul un crétin*)'," writes Badiou under his nom de plume, Georges Peyrol, acidly criticizing Deleuze and Deleuze's co-author Félix Guattari, "'can confuse the Marxist dialectical principle "One divides into two" with the genealogy for family ties concealed in "One becomes two"'."[30] Spurred on by what Badiou saw as Guattari's and Deleuze's non-fascist-proof rhizomatic ontology, Badiou sought a completely radical ontology which would forever stymie fascism. A splitting metaphysics which precluded all fascistic massing from the get-go became Badiou's philosophical and political obsession.[31]

Since May of 1968, Badiou has continuously refined his new ontology, eventually arriving at his proclamation in his 1988 *Being and Event* that mathematics is ontology.[32] What Badiou means

---

28 On the rhizome in Deleuze's thought, see Jonathan Dronsfield, "Deleuze and the Image of Thought," *Philosophy Today*, vol. 56, no. 4 (Nov., 2012).
29 Becky Vartabedian, *Multiplicity and Ontology in Deleuze and Badiou* (Cham, Switzerland: Palgrave Macmillan, 2018), p. 33, citing Georges Peyrol (Alain Badiou), "The Fascism of the Potato," p. 194
30 Becky Vartabedian, *Multiplicity and Ontology*, op. cit., p. 33, citing Georges Peyrol (Alain Badiou), "The Fascism of the Potato," p. 194
31 See also, e.g., Antonio Calcagno, "Fidelity to the Political Event: Hegel, Badiou, and the Return to the Same," in Jim Vernon and Antonio Calcagno, eds., *Badiou and Hegel: Infinity, Dialectics, Subjectivity* (Lanham, MD: Lexington Books, 2015), pp. 177-191.
32 "All that we know, and can ever know of being qua being, is set out, through the mediation of a theory of the pure multiple, by the historical

by this is different from what the early Pythagoreans and later neo-Pythagoreans understood as the primacy of number. Badiou's mathematics-as-ontology doctrine is the apotheosis of neo-neo-Pythagoreanism, the consummation of the numerification of the human person.

Unlike the Pythagoreans and neo-Pythagoreans, Badiou does not mean that numbers are the supreme mystery, or that calculation is a hint at the way the world operates, or that numerology provides a secret, Kabbalistic window into the hidden mechanics of a particular field of inquiry or the mind of God. What he means is that, quite literally, mathematics—specifically, set theory and subtraction—is Being itself. In the 2014 book *Mathematics of the Transcendental*, for example, Badiou sets forth, in great detail and using a smorgasbord of graphs, equations, and charts, how he sees mathematics as not just ruling the world, as the neo-Pythagoreans would have it, but *being* the world, giving the world existence—and that out of *no-thing* to boot.[33]

If Badiou is correct, then Fascism is indeed impossible. So is every other human activity besides Maoism. There can be no coalescing of human beings into Fascistic juggernauts on Badiou's neo-neo-Pythagorean reading, because, by their very nature, human beings are effervescences of non-being, unfungible and un-joinable under any political scheme but the masses-leading pronouncements of Mao. Herding the masses without claiming, as fascists are wont to do, to stand in their stead or to represent the group in their person, is all that can be expected, politically, from Badiou's mathematical ontology. And this is just as Badiou wants

---

discursivity of mathematics." Alain Badiou, tr. Oliver Feltham, *Being and Event* (London, UK: Continuum, 2006), p. 8

33   See, e.g., Alain Badiou, ed. and tr. A.J. Bartlett and Alex Ling, *Mathematics of the Transcendental* (London, UK: Bloomsbury, 2014), p. 145, also ibid., "Translators' Introduction: The Categorical Imperative," p. 5. See also A.J. Bartlett, "'Adjust Your Dread': Badiou's Metaphysical Disposition," in Abraham Jacob Greenstine and Ryan J. Johnson, eds., *Contemporary Encounters with Ancient Metaphysics* (Edinburgh, UK: Edinburgh University Press, 2017), esp. on what Bartlett calls Badiou's "metaphysics without metaphysics," p. 98.

it. Badiou has faced enormous criticism for both his political and philosophical views, and has adapted those views over time in response to critiques he found persuasive. But he has never substantially wavered in his insistence that mathematics is ontology, and that old-school communism of the Maoist variety is the only viable political approach.

To be sure, Badiou has faced more than just criticism and critique. Many have accused Badiou of ignorance of mathematics as a discipline. Critics have also found Badiou guilty of irresponsibility in applying mathematical concepts to philosophy—especially to metaphysics—in the way in which he does. For example, a 2011 essay by father-and-son authors Ricardo L. and David Nirenberg is a direct intervention into the inner workings of Badiou's proposed ontology. The Nirenbergs, to put it mildly, are not impressed with Badiou. They state flatly in the conclusion:

> Since Plato it has been the task of philosophy to help us distinguish, in their various contexts, between necessity and contingency. [...] Alain Badiou calls himself a Platonist and proclaims the revolutionary political power of his philosophy of numbers. [...] We can embrace the politics if we so wish. But we should not confuse this choice with mathematics, nor can we call it philosophy.[34]

And in their 1998 book *Fashionable Nonsense: Postmodern Intellectuals' Abuse of Science*, Alan Sokal and Jean Bricmont take Badiou to task for mashing up set theory, algebra, the "continuum hypothesis," the "filiation of coherence," and "trade-union realism" into what Sokal and Bricmont see as a hodgepodge of politics and "rather meaningless" mathematics.[35].

---

34   Ricardo L. Nirenberg and David Nirenberg, "Badiou's Number: A Critique of Mathematics as Ontology," *Critical Inquiry*, vol. 37 (Summer, 2011), p. 612

35   Alan Sokal and Jean Bricmont, *Fashionable Nonsense: Postmodern Intellectuals' Abuse of Science* (New York, NY: Picador, 1988), p. 181, see also footnotes 235 and 236. Sokal and Bricmont severely criticize Julia Kristeva for her apparent failure to understand set theory and mathematical logic more broadly. See Sokal and Bricmont, *Fashionable Nonsense*, op. cit., pp. 38-49. Badiou's fellow French philosopher, Jacques Lacan, comes in for especially abrupt

To be fair to Badiou, whether he is mistaken or not, his work is consciously grounded in the insights of some very important mathematical thinkers who came before him, as well as some other thinkers contemporary with Badiou. As Badiou himself repeatedly acknowledges in his various papers and books, he owes a particular intellectual debt to Gottlob Frege, Georg Cantor, Riemann, Bertrand Russell, John Von Neumann, and Richard Dedekind.[36] Badiou's critics fault Badiou for not deploying his forebears' ideas accurately, or for going beyond the bounds which those ideas permit. Badiou's critics may be right, but it is undeniable that Badiou himself is very much a part of the tradition of mathematical radicalism—late neo-Pythagoreanism, one might call it, or even proto-neo-neo-Pythagoreanism—which those thinkers established.[37]

Neo-Neo-Pythagoreanism: Big Data, Cyborgs, Transhumanism—What Next?

As I have argued above, it is possible to bracket Pythagoreanism, whatever it might have been, from the later and persistent pattern of ideas throughout the centuries—neo-Pythagoreanism—holding that numbers have some sort of secret constitutive or explanatory

---

critique for Lacan's use of integer theory and other mathematical-themed elements. Sokal and Bricmont, *Fashionable Nonsense*, op. cit., pp. 18-37.

36   See Alain Badiou, tr. Robin Mackay, *Number and Numbers* (Cambridge, UK: Polity, 2008), pp. 16-30 (Frege), 31-45 (Dedekind), 42-43 (Russell), 52-58 (Cantor), 67-72 (Von Neumann). On Riemann see, e.g., Becky Vartabedian, *Multiplicity and Ontology*, op. cit., pp. 57-69, Mirja Helena Hartimo, "Towards Completeness: Husserl on Theories of Manifolds 1890-1901," *Synthese*, vol. 156 (2007), pp. 281-301, and Marco Giovanelli, "The Forgotten Tradition: How the Logical Empiricists Missed the Philosophical Significance of the Work of Riemann, Christoffel, and Ricci," *Erkenntniss*, vol. 78 (2013), pp. 1219-1257.

37   It could be that in making the empty set generative of being Badiou is advancing a kind of Nishida Kitarō vision of Buddhist ontology, where in absolute nothingness (*zettai mu*) is somehow taken to be the ground of existence. See also on nothingness and Buddhist ontology Nishitani Keiji, tr. Graham Parkes and Setsuko Aihara, *The Self-Overcoming of Nihilism* (Albany, NY: State University of New York Press, 1990).

power. By the same token, it is also possible, for the purpose of this essay at least, to bracket the truth or falsehood of Badiou's mathematical ontology from the consequences of this way of thinking in the everyday world. Badiou may very well have been wrong when he said that mathematics is ontology. But in many ways Badiou's vision of reality is very close to how the contemporary world tends to operate. Ours is a decidedly Badiouist neo-neo-Pythagorean milieu. Our default mode of modern anthropology is not just that the universe is number, but that people are number, too.

Badiou can of course not be faulted for what would later be known as "digital Maoism" and the current plague of cancel culture and Twitter mobs.[38] The Internet and the online anti-society that we know today lay far in the future when Badiou was publishing broadsides against Deleuze, and then Deleuze and Guattari, beginning in the late 1960s.[39] But the digital Maoism of the present is an outgrowth of the empty-set Maoism of Badiou's early and then mature philosophical work, or at the very least a parallel to the thinking-of-being-as-number which is representative of Badiou's oeuvre. Badiou thought he was out-rhizoming Deleuze and Guattari by disaggregating aggregation from ontology, turning pure subtraction into the ground of (non-)being. Touché Jaron Lanier, who quoth, on the subject of Google and content: "The aggregator is richer than the aggregated." Maoism is now the biggest driver of stock prices on the planet. The numerification of the human person appears to be complete.

Perhaps the most eloquent exposition of and lament over what I am calling neo-neo-Pythagoreanism came out in 2019. Harvard Business School professor Shoshana Zuboff's book *The Age of Surveillance Capitalism* would be dystopian if it were not non-fiction.[40]

---

38   Jaron Lanier, "Digital Maoism: The Hazards of the New Online Collectivism," Edge, May 26, 2006. See also Rod Dreher, "Jaron Lanier & Digital Maoism," The American Conservative, Dec. 28, 2012

39   See Jason Morgan, "All the World Is Staged," *New Oxford Review*, May, 2021

40   *The Age of Surveillance Capitalism: The Fight for a Human Future at the New Frontier of Power* (New York, New York: Public Affairs, 2019)

In this book, Zuboff details how Google co-founders Sergey Brin and Larry Page, working with other Google engineers such as Amit Patel, hit upon a way to monetize their search engine using "data exhaust," or the traces of searches carried out by users of Google as they looked up movie names and dinner recipes, made flight and hotel reservations, and gradually offshored a myriad of other human cognitive exercises onto the Worldwide Web. Google executives were especially interested in shaping human behavior so that advertising—the mainstay of Internet companies' revenue in the early days of the online revolution—would no longer be necessary. Given the proper manipulation of human wants and even thoughts, people could be induced to buy things without the need for flashing banners and silly commercials.

Zuboff connects this (almost entirely unconsented-to) experiment in the terraforming of the human terrain to psychologist B.F. Skinner, whose 1948 book Walden Two was Skinner's program for turning people into functions of a social program. As I write elsewhere:

> In *Beyond Freedom and Dignity*, the work that preceded *Walden Two*, Skinner called for a "technology of behavior," which Skinner believed would lead to a new utopia by shaping our interior lives into one massive, pre-fabricated social order. This "utopia of certainty" is what Google, and its many imitators such as Facebook and Amazon, have commodified and marketed to advertisers as the most potent form of consumer mesmerization ever devised.[41]

Zuboff is concerned about the consequences of this "surveillance capitalism" for human society, in particular for democracy and the political ordering of human life. One could go farther and connect Zuboff's indictment of Google's practices to the radical "integerization" or "mathemicization" of human existence under

---

41   Jason Morgan, The New Structure of Sin: Mankind in the Age of Surveillance Capitalism," *Human Life Review*, vol. 46, no. 1 (Winter, 2000), p. 47

the neo-neo-Pythagorean regime. Badiou—and a fortiori those who came before him, such as Cantor and Riemann—of course did not intend the "surveillance capitalism" which was invented by Google executives and engineers in the late 1990s. But surveillance capitalism arguably could not have come about with the prior elevation of math itself to ontology by a long string of post-Cartesian anti-philosophers, and above all by French mathematical-Maoist Alain Badiou.

This "'integerization' or 'mathemicization' of human existence" is therefore traceable back at least to the Cartesian/Galilean mathematical turn mentioned above. For proto-neo-neo-Pythagoreans, humans became seen as cogs in a giant cosmic machine, or, if one really pushed the metaphor, as superfluous, even nefarious, interlopers in the cosmic clockwork. So pervasive has been the mathematization of ontology that the author of a book on "the physics of immortality" views the world as giant computer and eternity as a function of supercomputing.[42] The idea that the universe is a computer is not as fringe a theory as it sounds: some variation of the title "Are we living in a giant simulation?" has legs in online journalism.[43] This insistence on seeing ourselves as epiphenomena of a simulation, or more prosaically as avatars in an online world, has in turn helped usher in the now pervasive neo-neo-Pythagoreanism upon which the Internet and our modern hyper-connected life is predicated. By a strange series of turns from neo-Pythagoreanism to Baconian and Cartesian pseudo-science to dialectical materialism to algebraic ontology, we find ourselves today in the thrall of the algorithm, which, whether we realize it or not, works in human society on the principles of atomization and mathematical anthropology which Badiou has most consistently and forcefully explicat-

---

42   Frank Tipler, *The Physics of Immortality: Modern Cosmology, God and the Resurrection of the Dead* (New York, NY: Anchor Books, 1997)

43   One example: Caroline Delbert, "A Study Shows There's a 50% Chance We're Living in a Simulation," *Popular Mechanics*, Oct., 13, 2020. Things get weird quick: Leonard Susskind, "Dear Qubitzers, GR=QM," arXiv:1708.03040, Aug. 10, 2017. See also Giulio Prisco, "Simulation Physics and Theology for Qubitzers," Turing Church, Sept. 27, 2017.

ed. *Seul un crétin* could not see the steps from Badiou to Google to Amazon to Netflix.

In a troubling sense, this represents an overcoming, or overpowering, of the One/Many divide. We are all, on the neo-neo-Pythagorean scheme, both utterly solipsistic (an invincible One) and collectivized at random (an ever-latent Many).[44] Our age lurches between the two poles of isolation and hiving multiplicity which Badiou sought to embrace with his "empty set". Take transhumanism, for example, the package of notions that mankind is malleable, even transcendable, by technological innovation.[45] Transhumanism extends also to "solidarity with nonhuman people," as ecological Marxist Timothy Morton puts it, and to the socialist-utopian feminist cyborgism of Donna Haraway and her many followers.[46]

Theories much closer to the intellectual mainstream also betray neo-neo-Pythagorean tendencies a la the mathematical ontology of Alain Badiou. For example, economic-minded scholars have lamented the *homo economicus* model upon which so much of modern economics is based. Seen correctly, *homo economicus* is an Adam Smith and David Ricardo disciplinary fiction, a distortion of the human person into a calculating creature for the sake of economic "science." The set of economic assumptions broadly grouped under "Keynesianism" is also, on this reading, a function of seeing individuals not as unique but as aggregates of want and use, earning and consumption, with the average of those desires and exchanges expressed in currency notation at the behest of the currency-issuing central government bank.[47] These various economic paradigms are

---

44 See "Big Data," in Byung-Chul Han, *Psychopolitics: Neoliberalism and the New Technologies of Power* (London, England: Verso, 2017), pp. 55-76.

45 Ray Kurzweil, *The Singularity Is Near* (New York, NY: Viking, 2005)

46 Timothy Morton, Humankind: Solidarity with Nonhuman People (London: Verso, 2017) and Rebecca Pohl, An Analysis of Donna Haraway's A Cyborg Manifesto: *Science, Technology, and Socialist-Feminism in the Late Twentieth Century* (London: Routledge, 2018)

47 In this regard, Keynesianism and democracy are virtually interchangeable. See, e.g., Zachary D. Carter, *The Price of Peace: Money, Democracy, and the Life of John Maynard Keynes* (New York, NY: Random House, 2020). See also

potted in the same soil from which sprung Badiou's ontology of the empty set. Badiou did not invent neo-neo-Pythagoreanism, but he did bring it to its null-zenith.

It is surely in this malign spirit that we find the attempt by governments to manipulate entire groups of people as part of "population control," with the pernicious pseudo-science of eugenics deployed to aid the centers of political power in their mastery over people seen in terms of sheer number and not humanity.[48] Self-ownership, too, can rightly be seen as an attempt to rein in the social consequences of the "metaphysics without metaphysics" (see supra, note 33) of Badiou's empty-set ontology.[49] Even litera-

---

Ludwig von Mises, tr. H.E. Batson, *The Theory of Money and Credit* (New York, NY: Skyhorse, 2013), and Ludwig von Mises, *Human Action: A Treatise on Economics* (Auburn, Alabama: Ludwig von Mises Institute, 1998). See also "Does the Free Market Produce Free Persons?" in David L. Schindler, *Ordering Love: Liberal Societies and the Memory of God* (Grand Rapids, MI: William B. Eerdmans, 2011), pp. 154-165, John D. Mueller, *Redeeming Economics: Rediscovering the Missing Element* (Wilmington, DE: ISI Books, 2010), D.C. Schindler, *Freedom from Reality: The Diabolical Character of Modern Liberty* (Notre Dame, IN: University of Notre Dame Press, 2017), Mary Hirschfeld, *Aquinas and the Market: Toward a Humane Economy* (Cambridge, Massachusetts: Harvard University Press, 2018), and Christopher Ferrara, *Liberty, The God that Failed: Policing the Sacred and Constructing the Myths of the Secular State, from Locke to Obama* (Angelico Press, 2012).

48   See Obianuju Ekeocha, *Target Africa: Ideological Neocolonialism in the Twenty-First Century* (San Francisco, CA: Ignatius Press, 2018), Jason Morgan, "The Club of Rome in East Asia: U.S.-Led Population-Control Information Regimes and Waging the Cold War in the Far East," in Jason Morgan, ed., *Information Regimes during the Cold War in East Asia* (Oxon, England: Routledge, 2020), Steven W. Mosher, *Bully of Asia: Why China's Dream Is the New Threat to World Order* (Washington, DC: Regnery, 2017), and Jacqueline Kasun, *The War against Population: The Economics and Ideology of Population Control* (San Francisco, CA: Ignatius Press, 1988).

49   See, e.g., S. Adam Seagrave, "Self-Ownership vs. Divine Ownership: A Lockean Solution to a Liberal Democratic Dilemma," *American Journal of Political Science*, vol. 55, no. 3 (July, 2011), pp. 710-723, David Sobel, "Backing Away from Libertarian Self-Ownership," *Ethics*, vol. 123, no. 1 (October, 2012), pp. 32-60, and Edward Feser, "Self-Ownership, Abortion, and the Rights of Children: Toward a More Conservative Libertarianism," *Journal of Libertarian Studies*, vol. 18, no. 3 (Summer, 2004), pp. 91-114.

ture has suffered: László Bengi, for example, points to the influence of "calculation" in the creative writing of Franz Kafka.[50] Science, perhaps most of all, seems to have embraced what Thomas Kuhn called the distinction between observation and measurement, with some contemporary scientists moved to refute "digital ontology" in favor of "informational ontology" on the grounds that "the ultimate nature of reality is structural," and that "the universe is [not] a computational system equivalent to a Turing Machine".[51]

Conclusion

Human thought has long gravitated to numbers as explanations for at least some aspects of human existence. Until the rise of the modern state and the decoupling of the human person from the scientific enterprise (a decoupling greatly facilitated by the statistical, algebraic view of people as political units), this numerological tendency remained firmly subsumed within the wider sweep of philosophy as represented by the works of Plato and Aristotle. However, after the gradual destruction of science as philosophy started by anti-thinkers such as Galileo, Descartes, and Kant, the various strands of Pythagoreanism and neo-Pythagoreanism began to give way to neo-neo-Pythagoreanism, or the (mis-)understanding of the human person's very existence as a function of number.

This way of (not) thinking culminated with the literal mathematics-as-ontology doctrines of Alain Badiou. Under Badiou's scheme, an empty set stands in for metaphysics, which Badiou hopes will prevent the massification of individuals under a Fascist leader, but which in fact dissolves the human person into non-existence. The Big Data and Big Tech tyrannies which rule human societies in the present were not caused or foreseen by Badiou, but without his radical decoupling of human existence from any metaphysics or ontology, there would likely have been no finalization

---

50   László Bengi, "Calculation as a Cultural Practice in Modern Literature," *Neohelicon*, vol. 46 (2019), pp. 497-508
51   Luciano Floridi, "Against Digital Ontology," *Synthese*, no. 168 (2009), p. 151

of the neo-neo-Pythagorean trajectory—the dehumanizing "metaphysics without metaphysics"—such as we witness today.

Bibliography

Aktar, Md. Wasim and Dwaipayan Sengupta. 2011. "Fundamentals of Theoretical and Applied Mathematics: Role of Ancient Arabian and Egyptian Scientists". International Journal of Medical and Biological Frontiers, vol. 17, iss. 3.

Aristotle, ed. Richard McKeon. 1941. The Basic Works of Aristotle. New York, NY: Random House.

Badiou, Alain, tr. Oliver Feltham. 2006. Being and Event. London, UK: Continuum.

Badiou, Alain, ed. and tr. A.J. Bartlett and Alex Ling. 2014. Mathematics of the Transcendental. London, UK: Bloomsbury.

Badiou, Alain, tr. Robin Mackay. 2008. Number and Numbers. Cambridge, UK: Polity.

Badiou, Alain, with Gilles Haéri, tr. Susan Spitzer. 2016. In Praise of Mathematics. Cambridge, UK: Polity.

Bartlett, A.J. 2017. "'Adjust Your Dread': Badiou's Metaphysical Disposition". In Abraham Jacob Greenstine and Ryan J. Johnson, eds., Contemporary Encounters with Ancient Metaphysics. Edinburgh, UK: Edinburgh University Press.

Bealer, George. 1987. "The Philosophical Limits of Scientific Essentialism". Philosophical Perspectives, vol. 1, Metaphysics.

Bengi, László. 2019. "Calculation as a Cultural Practice in Modern Literature". Neohelicon, vol. 46.

Blankinship, Kevin. 2020. "Suffering the Sons of Eve: Animal Ethics in al-Ma'arrī's Epistle of the Horse and the Mule". Religions, vol. 11.

Bowra, Cecil Maurice. 1957. The Greek Experience. Cleveland.

Bradley, M.C. 2002. "The Fine-Tuning Argument: The Bayesian Version". Religious Studies, vol. 38.

Brentano, Franz. 1999. "The Four Phases of Philosophy and Its Present Condition". Philosophy Today, vol. 43, no. 1.

Calcagno, Antonio. 2015. "Fidelity to the Political Event: Hegel, Badiou, and the Return to the Same". In Jim Vernon and Antonio Calcagno, eds., Badiou and Hegel: Infinity, Dialectics, Subjectivity. Lanham, MD: Lexington Books.

Carter, Zachary D. 2020. The Price of Peace: Money, Democracy, and the Life of John Maynard Keynes. New York, NY: Random House.

Celenza, Christopher S. 1999. "Pythagoras in the Renaissance: The Case of Marsilio Ficino". Renaissance Quarterly, vol. 52, no. 3.

Cornelli, Gabrielle. 2016. "A Review of Aristotle's Claim Regarding Pythagoreans['] Fundamental Beliefs: All Is Number?" Filosofia Unisinos: Unisinos Journal of Philosophy, vol. 17, no. 1.

Cornelli, Gabrielle. 2015. "Review of Phillip Sidney Horky, Plato and Pythagoreanism (Oxford University Press, 2013)". American Journal of Philology, vol. 136.

Curd, Patricia. 2011. "New Work on the Presocratics". Journal of the History of Philosophy, vol. 49, no. 1.

Das, Aileen R. 2019. "Probable New Fragments and a Testimonium on Galen's Commentary on Plato's Timaevs". The Classical Quarterly, vol. 69, no. 1.

Delbert, Caroline. 2020. "A Study Shows There's a 50% Chance We're Living in a Simulation". Popular Mechanics.

Delfino, Robert A. 2014. "The Cultural Dangers of Scientism and Common Sense Solutions". Studia Gilsoniana, vol. 3 (supplement).

Dreher, Rod. 2012. "Jaron Lanier & Digital Maoism." The American Conservative.

Dronsfield, Jonathan. 2012. "Deleuze and the Image of Thought". Philosophy Today, vol. 56, no. 4.

Ekeocha, Obianuju. 2018. Target Africa: Ideological Neocolonialism in the Twenty-First Century. San Francisco, CA: Ignatius Press.

Ferrara, Christopher. 2012. Liberty, The God that Failed: Policing the Sacred and Constructing the Myths of the Secular State, from Locke to Obama. Angelico Press.

Feser, Edward. 2004. "Self-Ownership, Abortion, and the Rights of Children: Toward a More Conservative Libertarianism". Journal of Libertarian Studies, vol. 18, no. 3.

Floridi, Luciano. 2009. "Against Digital Ontology". Synthese, no. 168.

Foucault, Michel. Discipline and Punish: The Birth of the Prison. New York, NY: Random House.

Giovanelli, Marco. 2013. "The Forgotten Tradition: How the Logical Empiricists Missed the Philosophical Significance of the Work of Riemann, Christoffel, and Ricci". Erkenntniss, vol. 78.

Goldin, Owen. 2015. "The Pythagorean Table of Opposites, Symbolic Classification, and Aristotle". Science in Context, vol. 28, no. 2.

Grant, Edward. 2007. A History of Natural Philosophy: From the Ancient World to the Nineteenth Century. Cambridge, England: Cambridge University Press.

Guicciardini, Niccolò. 2013. "The Role of Musical Analogies in Newton's Optical and Cosmological Work". Journal of the History of Ideas, vol. 74, no. 1.

Han, Byung-Chul. 2018. The Expulsion of the Other. Cambridge, England: Polity Press.

Han, Byung-Chul. 2017. Psychopolitics: Neoliberalism and the New Technologies of Power. London, England: Verso.

Hancock, Curtis L. 2015. "The One and the Many: The Ontology of Science in Aristotle and Thomas Aquinas". The Review of Metaphysics, vol. 69, no. 2.

Hancock, Curtis L. 2012. "The Nature of Metaphysics and

Science: The Problem of the One and the Many in Thomas Aquinas". In Mark Pestana, ed., Metaphysics. Rijeka: InTech Publishing.

Hartimo, Mirja Helena. 2007. "Towards Completeness: Husserl on Theories of Manifolds 1890-1901". Synthese, vol. 156.

Hellman, Geoffrey. 1981. "How to Gödel a Frege-Russell: Gödel's Incompleteness Theorems and Logicism". Noûs, vol. 15, no. 4.

Higgs, Edward. 2004. The Information State in England: The Central Collection of Information on Citizens since 1500. Hampshire, England: Palgrave Macmillan.

Hirschfeld, Mary. 2018. Aquinas and the Market: Toward a Humane Economy. Cambridge, Massachusetts. Harvard University Press.

Huffman, Carl. 2019. "Pythagoras and Isis". The Classical Quarterly, vol. 69, no. 2.

Hunter, Ian. 2016. "Heideggerian Mathematics: Badiou's Being and Event as Spiritual Pedagogy". Representations, no. 134.

Ikeda Yoshiaki. 2018. Nishida Kitarō no jitsuzairon: AI, andoroido wa naze ningen wo koerarenai no ka. Tokyo: Akashi.

Johnston, Adrian. 2009. "The Right Left: Alain Badiou and the Disruption of Political Identities". Yale French Studies, no. 116/117.

Joost-Gaugier, Christiane L. 2006. Measuring Heaven: Pythagoras and His Influence on Thought and Art in Antiquity and the Middle Ages. Ithaca, NY: Cornell University Press.

Kang, Minsoo. 2007. "The Mechanical Daughter of Rene Descartes: The Origin and History of an Intellectual Fable". Modern Intellectual History, vol. 14, no. 3.

Kasun, Jacqueline. 1988. The War against Population: The Economics and Ideology of Population Control. San Francisco, CA: Ignatius Press.

Kukkonen, Taneli. 2015. "Review of Peter Adamson and Peter E. Portman, eds. and trs., The Philosophical Works of al-Kindī, Oxford-New York: Oxford University Press, 2012". Journal of the History of Philosophy, vol. 53, no. 3.

Kurzweil, Ray. 2005. The Singularity Is Near. New York, NY: Viking.

Kutz, Christopher. 2002. "The Collective Work of Citizenship". Legal Theory, vol. 8.

Lanier, Jaron. 2006. "Digital Maoism: The Hazards of the New Online Collectivism". Edge.

Lloyd, David R. 2010. "Symmetry and Beauty in Plato". Symmetry, vol. 2.

Mazour-Matsusevitch, Yelena. 2014. "(Neo)Pythagorean Vision in Thomas More's Utopia". Moreana, vol. 51, nos. 195&196.

McMurran, Mary-Helen. 2019. "Locke's Mythical Thinking: Metempsychosis in the Theory of Personal Identity".

ELH, vol. 86.

Morgan, Jason. 2021. "All the World Is Staged". New Oxford Review.

Morgan, Jason. 2020. "The Club of Rome in East Asia: U.S.-Led Population-Control Information Regimes and Waging the Cold War in the Far East". In Jason Morgan, ed., Information Regimes during the Cold War in East Asia. Oxon, England: Routledge.

Morgan, Jason. 2020. "Review of Shoshana Zuboff, The Age of Surveillance Capitalism". Human Life Review, vol. 46, no. 1.

Morton, Timothy. 2017. Humankind: Solidarity with Nonhuman People. London, England: Verso.

Mosher, Steven W. 2017. Bully of Asia: Why China's Dream Is the New Threat to World Order. Washington, DC: Regnery.

Mueller, John D. 2010. Redeeming Economics: Rediscovering the Missing Element. Wilmington, DE: ISI Books.

Nirenberg, Ricardo L. and David Nirenberg. 2011. "Badiou's Number: A Critique of Mathematics as Ontology". Critical Inquiry, vol. 37.

Nishitani Keiji, tr. Graham Parkes and Setsuko Aihara. 1990. The Self-Overcoming of Nihilism. Albany, NY: State University of New York Press.

Oprea, Alexandra. 2019. "Pluralism and the General Will: The Roman and Spartan Models in Rousseau's Social Contract".

The Review of Politics, vol. 81.

O'Rourke, Fran. 1992. Pseudo-Dionysius and the Metaphysics of Aquinas. Notre Dame, IN: University of Notre Dame Press.

Owens, Joseph. 1959. A History of Ancient Western Philosophy. New York, NY: Appleton-Century-Crofts.

Pohl, Rebecca. 2018. An Analysis of Donna Haraway's A Cyborg Manifesto: Science, Technology, and Socialist-Feminism in the Late Twentieth Century. London, England: Routledge.

Povilionienè, Rima. 2017. "Musica Fibonacciana: Aesthetic and Practical Approach". New Sound, vol. 50, no. II.

Prisco, Giulio. 2017. "Simulation Physics and Theology for Qubitzers". Turing Church.

Raattkainen, Panu. 2005. "On the Philosophical Relevance of Gödel's Incompleteness Theorems". Revue Internationale de Philosophie, vol. 4.

Redpath, Peter A. 2012. A Not-So-Elementary Christian Metaphysics. Manitou Springs, CO: Socratic Press.

Redpath, Peter A. 1999. "Why Descartes Was Not a Philosopher. In Brendan Sweetman, ed., The Failure of Modernism: The Cartesian Legacy and Contemporary Pluralism. Mishawaka, Indiana: American Maritain Association.

Reinhardt, William N. 1985. "Absolute Versions of Incompleteness Theorems". Noûs, vol. 19, no. 3.

Roberts, Siobhan. 2016. "Waiting for Gödel". The New Yorker, June 29.

Robichaud, Denis. 2015. "Review of David Albertson, Mathematical Theologies: Nicholas of Cusa and the Legacy of Theirry of Chartres, Oxford Studies in Historical Theology, New York, NY: Oxford University Press, 2014". Journal of the History of Philosophy, vol. 53, no. 2.

Salmon, Wesley C. 1998. "A Contemporary Look at Zeno's Paradoxes: An Excerpt from Space, Time, and Motion". In Peter van Inwagen and Dean W. Zimmerman, eds. Metaphysics: The Big Questions. Malden, MA: Blackwell.

Scarpelli, Therese and Staff. 2006. "Review of Carl A. Huffman, Archytas of Tarentum: Pythagorean, Philosopher, and Mathematician King, Cambridge: Cambridge University Press, 2005". The Review of Metaphysics, vol. 60, no. 2.

Schindler, David L. 2011. Ordering Love: Liberal Societies and the Memory of God. Grand Rapids, MI: William B. Eerdmans.

Schindler, D.C. 2017. Freedom from Reality: The Diabolical Character of Modern Liberty. Notre Dame, IN: University of Notre Dame Press.

Seagrave, S. Adam. 2011. "Self-Ownership vs. Divine Ownership: A Lockean Solution to a Liberal Democratic Dilemma". American Journal of Political Science, vol. 55, no. 3.

Sobel, David. 2012. "Backing Away from Libertarian Self-Ownership". Ethics, vol. 123, no. 1.

Shapiro, Stewart. 2002. "Incompleteness and Inconsistency". Mind, vol. 111, no. 444.

Sutton, John. 2003. "Review of Dennis Des Chene, Spirits and Clocks: Machine and Organism in Descartes (Ithaca and London: Cornell University Press, 2001)". British Journal for the History of Science.

Slaveva-Griffin, Svetla. 2014. "Review of J. Kalvesmaki, The Theology of Arithmetic: Number Symbolism in Platonism and Early Christianity (Hellenic Studies 59), Washington, DC: Center for Hellenic Studies, 2013". The Classical Review, vol. 64, no. 2.

Sokal, Alan and Jean Bricmont. 1988. Fashionable Nonsense: Postmodern Intellectuals' Abuse of Science. New York, NY: Picador.

Starr, S. Frederick. 2013. Lost Enlightenment: Central Asia's Golden Age from the Arab Conquest to Tamerlane. Princeton, NJ: Princeton University Press.

Steinberger, Peter J. 2008. "Hobbes, Rousseau and the Modern Conception of the State". The Journal of Politics, vol. 70, no. 3.

Susskind, Leonard. 2017. "Dear Qubitzers, GR=QM". arXiv:1708.03040.

TeSelle, Eugene. 1997. "Review of Alastair H.B. Logan, Gnostic Truth and Christian Heresy: A Study in the History of Gnosticism". Church History, vol. 66, no. 3.

Tipler, Frank. 1997. The Physics of Immortality: Modern Cosmology, God and the Resurrection of the Dead. New York, NY: Anchor Books.

Vartabedian, Becky. 2018. Multiplicity and Ontology in Deleuze and Badiou. Cham, Switzerland: Palgrave Macmillan.

von Mises, Ludwig, tr. H.E. Batson. 1998. The Theory of Money and Credit. New York, NY: Skyhorse.

von Mises, Ludwig. 1998. Human Action: A Treatise on Economics. Auburn, Alabama: Ludwig von Mises Institute.

Weirich, Paul. 1986. "Rousseau on Proportional Majority Rule". Philosophy and Phenomenological Research, vol. 47, no. 1.

Whitehead, Alfred North. 1978 (1929). Process and Reality. New York, NY: MacMillan.

Zhmud, Leonid J. 1989. "'All Is Number?' Basic Doctrine of Pythagoreanism Reconsidered". Phronesis, vol. 34.

Zuboff, Shoshana. 2019. The Age of Surveillance Capitalism: The Fight for a Human Future at the New Frontier of Power. New York, New York: Public Affairs.

Essays and Book Reviews

Exploring a Roadmap Toward Biblical Reconciliation

Christopher Croom

General Introduction

Christians live in confusing times in 2021 America. The tremendous push of Social Justice (SJ) is increasingly influential in media, politics, and culture. The SJ push is so strong that it is causing deep division in the culture and the Church as well.[1] Christian denominations find themselves on the verge of splitting, while ministries who experience fewer extreme conditions still struggle to find a biblical balance to respond to the calls for change. For those Churches and Church Leaders who take the moderate position: what does the Bible have to provide you as a roadmap to direct your pathway? For Scholars writing to edify the Church: how can we put Churches and Christians on the narrow path?

What seems to be clear at this juncture is that one side of America feels the perceived sting of decades of systemic injustice and believes restitution and reconciliation must be made. On the other hand, the second half feels that nothing is to be done because they were not the direct antagonist. This paper will likely not convince either side to change their position. However, it may reach those in a middle group if such a group exists.

The purpose of this editorial then aims to discuss a clearer understanding of the socially relevant elements of a social and religious middle ground through the study of the Epistle to Philemon and the structure and procedure of biblical reconciliation between

---

1   "U.S. Church Membership Falls Below Majority for First Time," accessed July 8, 2021, https://news.gallup.com/poll/341963/church-membership-falls-below-majority-first-time.aspx.

the perceived oppressed and perceived oppressor. Additionally, this work will review some recent publications written around this topic and position itself in a more reasonable and actionable position for the middle ground. Ultimately, this work will draw a roadmap for those who wish to engage in better discussions on the subject of social justice and reconciliation.

This paper will start by introducing the first nine verses of Philemon, paying close attention to the relation between Paul (the advocate) and Philemon (the perceived oppressor). From there, we will review potential positions for understanding the text. The author has chosen to work in this order to ensure there is a basic understanding of the epistle before other opinions are brought to bear.

Working through the heart of the text will be the next task taken on. Verses ten through twenty-five will be examined, paying particular attention to the relationship between Paul and Onesimus and Paul's intercession on the latter's behalf. In closing, two sections will be presented: The penultimate will address the silence of Onesimus in the text and its relevancy. This section of the work will be vitally important to bridge the gap from Biblical text to Cultural applicability.

Textual Introduction

The well-known Apostle, Paul, here introduces himself with unique terminology. Nowhere else in the New Testament will you find Paul introduce himself with the word δέσμιος. Referring to himself as a *prisoner* of the Lord may both reflect the current state of Paul, being imprisoned in Rome, as well as an intimation toward Philemon, as Paul prepares to appeal on behalf of Onesimus; alternatively, it could explain to Philemon why Paul did not make the trip himself and why he believes Onesimus may be helpful to him.[2] Dunn notes that Paul shies away from "pulling rank" by naming himself as an Apostle and instead opts for a more direct and person-

---

2   Richard R. Melick, Philippians, Colossians, Philemon, vol. 32, *The New American Commentary* (Nashville: Broadman & Holman Publishers, 1991), 349.

al greeting to open this letter.³ Paul additionally seems to greet the entire family and household of Philemon by referring to Apphia (his wife) and Archippus (his son) and the Church in their home. The Church in the home of Philemon would undoubtedly, as was tradition, include those household slaves within their presence.⁴

Fascinatingly, verses one through nine seem to be an inclusion in the text. If scrutinized, verses one and nine both allude to Paul as a prisoner while making clear an appeal is coming. Verses two and eight seem loosely connected because a decision affecting the entire family and household needs to be made. Paul addressing the wife and son of Philemon alongside the Church in their house appears to be a calculated move by Paul, and verse eight appears to shed light on why that may be plausible. While this author recognizes this as primarily an argument from silence, it is nevertheless curious that Paul opens this decision to insight from those around Philemon.

Verses three and seven point to the blessing received by each party; one a blessing from God, indirectly through Paul's desire, and the other the blessing Paul receives through the ministry of Philemon to the Church in his home. Douglas Moo notates that the term "grace and peace" that Paul employs is both theology significant as the gifts that God gives through the Gospel, but also points to this as "a way of summarizing the universal "well-being" (shalōm) that God would establish in the last days."⁵

Verses four and six highlight the prayers of Paul. The first, in verse four, recounts the thanksgiving of Paul as he continues to intercede on behalf of this Church and family. Paul is taking the

---

3   James D. G. Dunn, *The Epistles to the Colossians and to Philemon: A Commentary on the Greek Text*, New International Greek Testament Commentary (Grand Rapids, MI; Carlisle: William B. Eerdmans Publishing; Paternoster Press, 1996), 310.
4   Peter Gorday, ed., *Colossians, 1–2 Thessalonians, 1–2 Timothy, Titus, Philemon*, Ancient Christian Commentary on Scripture (Downers Grove, IL: InterVarsity Press, 2000), 310.
5   Douglas J. Moo, *The Letters to the Colossians and to Philemon*, The Pillar New Testament Commentary (Grand Rapids, MI: William B. Eerdmans Pub. Co., 2008), 384.

time to establish his love for this family. As this paper begins to dive deeper, it will become clear why Paul needs to clear the air with Philemon before addressing the issue at hand. These two verses, alongside verse five, are the heart of this introduction. Melick points out that these three verses create "logical (thematic) patterns of thanksgiving and prayer."[6] What is noteworthy to point out as we investigate verse five is that Paul's prayers that surround this verse are said to be prayers that seek out Philemon's continued activity and fruitfulness.

Paul is inclined to make this intercession because Philemon displays a love and faith toward God, which spills out over and onto the Church. However, what he also does is build a bridge to his upcoming appeal. He characterizes and praises Philemon for his Christianity toward Christians. Here, Paul employs three forms of rhetoric to lay the foundation for what might come.

In no particular order, Paul begins with the first, *ethos*. In this letter, Paul establishes that These men are all fellow workers of the Gospel, with God in common. Their callings revolve around the glory of God, based upon what God has done in their own lives. Thus, their actions and responses belonged not to their autonomy but rather to God's sovereignty. Christians are called to submit to the will of God and to love the brethren. Paul establishes a reasonable and ethical fact to begin: We have been established as newly created, requiring a new standard of living, and Paul appeals to that new character.

From that point, Paul can further establish *pathos*. The pulling of the heartstrings is an effective form of communication. The Apostle uses emotional language in verse five, such as love and faith, and points of the direct objects of that love and faith—God and the Saints of God. While this author continues to hold that Onesimus was a runaway slave and thief (despite some of the more modern positions), there is little doubt that Philemon is dis-

---

6   Richard R. Melick, *Philippians, Colossians, Philemon, vol. 32, The New American Commentary* (Nashville: Broadman & Holman Publishers, 1991), 351.

appointed at the actions of Onesimus. The Apostle Paul looks to quell that emotional state of Philemon by replacing it with another emotional consideration.

Finally, you can see Paul's use of *logos* as well. The logical conclusion of all that he has said in these opening verses should point to Philemon being able to see this situation from a perspective outside of his initial emotions and through the lens of Christ's Gospel. If Christ has forgiven and called Philemon to use in the work of the Gospel, so then might Onesimus be worthy of such consideration from his master. However, does Philemon genuinely have a right to be upset with Onesimus? Is Onesimus whom we think he is?

Potential Positions on Philemon

D.F. Tolmie, Professor of Old and New Testament studies at the University of the Free State, South Africa, presented a couple of fascinating alternative positions. Tolmie indeed acknowledges that the popular interpretation of Philemon is one of a culprit, saved by Paul. Tolmie cites the work of Chrysostom and Theodore of Mopsuestia of the Early Church Fathers (ECFs) and their particular view of this useless runaway slave.[7] However, as time moves forward, Tolmie identifies other interpretations of this letter and the circumstances that may have birthed them.

In discussing abolishing the slave trade in Britain in 1807 and the Abolition Act of 1833, Tolmie discusses how the debates on slavery were often theological and favored those who defended slavery, saying, "In this debate, the Letter to Philemon was often used, and, in a theological world dominated by a literal approach to the Bible, 'the pro-slavery arguments often had the better case' (Barclay 2007:13).' In fact, the argument was deceptively simple: that Paul sent a runaway slave back to his master proves that slavery was an institution willed by God."[8]

---

[7] D. F. Tolmie, "How Onesimus Was Heard – Eventually. Some Insights from the History of Interpretation of Paul's Letter to Philemon," *Acta Theologica* 2019 (July 22, 2019): 101–117.

[8] Ibid.

Now, we have already examined the first half of the text. From this, this author sees no reason to assume Paul was arguing for continued slavery or even evidencing that he was ok with the idea of enslaving another man. The only thing that is abundantly clear is that Paul was appealing to Philemon in various methods to prepare to ask something of him—something we will examine shortly.

However, expanding on Tolmie's potential understanding is the Rev. Obusitswe Tiroyabone. Tiroyabone believes that the text needs to be read through the lens of the oppressed party (Onesimus) rather than the oppressors (Paul and Philemon).[9] Moreover, Tiroyabone suggests "that these [interpreting] scholars write from the perspective of the beneficiaries of both the colonial and postcolonial eras."[10] Between Tolmie and Tiroyabone, it appears that they have created a metanarrative from total silence and given Onesimus a character, intellect, and plan that one would struggle to find in the text.

> Onesimus needs to be liberated from the traditional runaway-slave hypothesis; he has been misrepresented and needs to be called out as an intelligent person who was oppressed by a system of slavery and used that system to liberate himself from it.[11]

Tiroyabone continues by declaring that the traditional position suppresses the "intelligence, worth, capacity to think, and importance" of Onesimus, all while ignoring his capacity of self-liberation.[12]

Adding more possibilities to what we read in the epistle, Jennifer Glancy considers the power dynamic in the exchange and how Paul and Philemon may be implicitly using Philemon as a pawn in the work of their respective ministries. Recalling some of her re-

---

[9] Rev Obusitswe Tiroyabone, "Reading Philemon with Onesimus in the Postcolony: Exploring a Postcolonial Runaway Slave Hypothesis," *Acta Theologica* 36 (2016): 225–236.
[10] Ibid.
[11] Ibid.
[12] Ibid.

search, Glancy notes that, "Perhaps Paul characterises [sic] Onesimus as ἄχρηστος, ineffective, because he has failed in the mission on which he was sent, a mission intended to establish Philemon as Paul's patron... I will argue that the recipients of the letter would have understood ἄχρηστος as 'disposable,' with some similar implications."[13] Glancy believes Onesimus's usefulness only extends to his position as a pawn in the negotiations of Philemon and Paul. Thus, it would appear that Tolmie, Tiroyabone, and Glancy are all reading the Apostle's epistle with the same tint—in that they are reading something counter-cultural (to us) into the text. As one considers these claims from the authors mentioned above, one must consider not just the culture but, first and foremost, the theology. Therefore, to properly examine the veracity of these hypotheses, we need to examine the biblical text further to see if we can find any evidence to strengthen their positions.

Advancing the Text

Verses ten through twenty-five present the much-anticipated appeal of Paul. We will focus on verses ten through twenty-one only, but in two parts—first, verses ten through sixteen, discussing the direct request from Paul. Then, to finish our exegetical discussion, we will review and examine verses seventeen through twenty-one.

Paul appeals or *encourages* Philemon to hear him out, regarding Onesimus, whom Paul identifies as his τέκνου. It would seem to this author that Paul's use of a word so closely related to biological posterity, in a spiritual sense, would signify a filial relationship that would go beyond simply using Onesimus as a pawn in a scheme. The term τέκνου is used 40 times in the Gospels alone, and many of those times by Christ. It would seem that Paul is borrowing language from Christ as he employs this terminology another 39 times in his writings in the New Testament. In many instances, such as Rom 8:16, 17; 1 Cor 4:14; 2 Cor 6:13; Gal 4:19; Eph 5:1; Php

---

13   Jennifer A. Glancy, "The Utility of an Apostle: On Philemon 11," *Journal of Early Christian History* 5, no. 1 (January 2015): 72–86.

2:15; Col 3:21, Paul uses this term to talk about children who are expected to take after their named father in some way. These many passages illustrate an expectation that symbolizes closeness and similarity between the father and the son. Paul clearly introduces Onesimus into the epistle by explaining that a change has occurred in him resulting from Paul's evangelistic efforts toward him.

Yet, Tolmie, Tiroyabone, and Glancy all prefer a reading that disacknowledges Paul's direct labeling of Onesimus as a son, and his evangelistic rhetoric, evidencing a closeness between the two. It is curious to determine why this language was glossed over in all three essays. It would seem to this author that this text may have been read by those authors anachronistically, employing modern-day considerations over an ancient text.

However, the central question of the text lies in verse eleven (it will also help us address the previous claims of the three authors as mentioned above). We briefly discussed the use of ἄχρηστος and εὔχρηστος, but up until this point, it has been a cursory examination, and generally the opinion of other scholars put forth. At this point, Glancy's research of Marchal should also be introduced. "For Marchal… Paul's designation of Onesimus as ἄχρηστος and εὔχρηστος necessarily evokes the ubiquitous sexual use of slaves."[14] From a practical standpoint, though Glancy notes Marchal's reference to using these words in places like Romans 1:26 27 in that manner, it is unthinkable for Paul first to introduce Onesimus as his *child*, then introduce such provocative language regarding his utility. This occurrence would be a contradiction of thought in how Paul instructs Christians regarding the family structure and his reverence for the husband-and-wife unit located elsewhere in his epistles (most notably 1 Corinthians 7).

What Tolmie, Tiroyabone, and especially Glancy (via Marchal) miss in this text is a critical piece of information that is noted by James Dunn, as he explains, "Onesimus" means literally "useful." This allows Paul the appropriate pun, though if the experience of

---

14   Ibid.

those whose names allow such puns today is anything to go by, Onesimus must have been heartily sick of it by this time."[15]

In all likelihood, Onesimus was a slave under the authority of Philemon, who never lived up to the work he was in place to do. This play on words from Paul likely points to the idea that this once 'unprofitable and unhelpful' slave (whose was even *named* to be helpful), is now, by the grace of God, a brother in the work to be done, and should be reevaluated upon his return as one who is profitable for the work of the ministry. While slavery is seen as an unsavory practice to our modern eyes and ears, there is a dichotomy that must be made concerning how slavery is discussed in the Bible.

In the Old Testament, the people of Israel were both slaves and slave-owners. Douglas Wilson explains the difference skillfully, noting that the slavery instituted by the Mosaic law was more like an indentured servanthood or a bond apprenticeship. Conversely, there was a slavery implemented by a wicked, God-hating world; pagans, who are their own measure of rule and law.[16] This statement is understandably a hard pill for many to swallow. However, the modern mind is quick to forget that our general employment agreement with our employer is similar to this structure. While there are significant differences, the basic framework remains the same, and this construct should be given deep consideration before dismissing it entirely.

The appeal that Paul now builds upon is based upon a twofold premise. The first premise is that *Onesimus is different*. This runaway slave is no longer lazy, unprofitable, and undisciplined. Onesimus has had an *experience* that has fundamentally changed

---

15   James D. G. Dunn, The Epistles to the Colossians and to Philemon: A Commentary on the Greek Text, New International Greek Testament Commentary (Grand Rapids, MI; Carlisle: William B. Eerdmans Publishing; Paternoster Press, 1996), 328–329.
16   Douglas Wilson, *Black & Tan: A Collection of Essays and Excursions on Slavery, Culture War, and Scripture in America* (Moscow, ID: Canon Press, 2005), 38.

the way he sees the world and the opportunities that lay before him. The second premise is that *Onesimus has given evidence of this change by his actions*. Onesimus has taken this opportunity to assimilate himself into the Church's mission, particularly Paul's care.

Paul begins verse thirteen by saying he "ἐβουλόμην" to keep Onesimus with him. The use of this imperfect verb reflects that Paul gave deep consideration on whether to send the once useless slave back to his master or not; Paul "was wanting" to keep Onesimus by his side because of the change that came over him and made him useful to the ministry; Paul says that Onesimus is ministering to him in his imprisonment. This fact alone indicates assimilation has occurred in the life of Onesimus, and he is no longer whom he used to be.

Moreover, Paul continues to employ language that evidences this fact. Paul acknowledges the sovereignty of God in removing Onesimus from the home of Philemon for the purpose of turning him into a servant of the Gospel. Paul now indicates a significant change of relationship ought to occur because of God's work. In verses fifteen to sixteen, it is stated that his removal was to change the status of his relationship with his former master: Onesimus should come back, but not as a δοῦλον, but instead as ἀδελφὸν. This relationship change from slave to beloved brother would not be possible without assimilating into a new house and a new way of life.

However, what of the wrong that Onesimus has committed against Philemon? What about the theft of property before he abdicated duty and service? Paul says, "τοῦτο ἐμοὶ ἐλλόγα," charge me. The point of Paul's request was not to pay for the wrong of Onesimus; it instead might be said in our everyday language to count this as "water under the bridge," because certainly, Philemon *would not charge* anything to Paul.

The Voice of Onesimus through an Advocate

Looking again to Tolmie, we find he believes that Paul being the voice of Onesimus was not only for the benefit of the former slave but also and possibly predominantly, for his own benefit.[17] Moreover, Tolmie says,

> Christianity often has noble ideas, but that these should be tested by what happens in practice. For example, in the American context, the European Christians' sense of superiority was merely fostered and reinforced. Something similar happened in the interpretation of the Letter to Philemon. Onesimus was never taken as the starting point for interpreting the letter; only Paul's voice was heard.[18]

This statement is dubious on its face. As we have examined, the reality of this letter s that Paul is making an explicit appeal on behalf of someone who did not previously have a voice. Thus, as has *always* been the case, an advocate has always been required as men assimilate from the world of slavery into a new system. While many may say this is the transition of a slave, out of slavery, into the system that enslaved him, it is also, paradoxically, the system that allows men to become free; Onesimus is the very proof.

The change in citizenship is now a reality for Onesimus. Paul leans on that shared citizenship in that it would be determinative for the new relationship between the two.[19] However, Tolmie continues to believe that Onesimus's brotherhood continues to be disingenuous until he is no longer seen as a threat and is allowed to speak on his own behalf. [20] The frustration for this author (while

---

17   Tolmie, "How Onesimus Was Heard – Eventually. Some Insights from the History of Interpretation of Paul's Letter to Philemon."
18   Ibid.
19   James D. G. Dunn, *The Epistles to the Colossians and to Philemon: A Commentary on the Greek Text, New International Greek Testament Commentary* (Grand Rapids, MI; Carlisle: William B. Eerdmans Publishing; Paternoster Press, 1996), 335.
20   Ibid.

being an inherent benefit for Tolmie) of this position is that Onesimus has left us nothing of his speech. So, if we continue to believe Onesimus cannot be assimilated into new citizenship until his voice is heard, we will never have the evidence to move forward in his story. It seems to be duplicitous of Tolmie to present a problem that has no solution, rather than investigate the evidence that is available to us, and such seems to be the stance of many modern-day warriors of perceived "social justice."

Speaking Directly to the Culture

So, how do we take this exegetical evidence before us in the Epistle to Philemon and find a moral principle to help build a cultural ethic? Well, we must take the moral principles available to us in the story.

What we know is that Paul reminded Philemon of the ministry they shared in, in caring for the people of God. He then presents Onesimus as someone whom God has claimed for Himself and entered into His citizenship. Upon this assimilation, Onesimus has become helpful and productive in the kingdom economy. This can only happen by embracing the kingdom principles of the citizenry, and this is the principle we can pass on to those who want to understand better what reconciliation looks like on a national level. Moreover, this will enlighten those who wonder what truly stands in the way of authentic justice in the polis.

While there is no doubt the Gospel is the source of spiritual reconciliation to God and peace within Christianity, as those whom God calls to preserve peace and truth in the world in which we live, we must ask ourselves by what principles we can produce as much peace as we can in the world in which we exist? In other words, "what is the best public policy, based on biblical principle we can all live by?"

I believe that a history of racism in America and its lasting effects (even when systemically halted by law) must be acknowledged by those it has not historically affected. I believe in many ways *it has been* acknowledged. Through organizations and programs designed to help people of color progress, there have certainly been strides made. On the other hand, people of color supporting radical change must acknowledge the hypocrisy of what they are saying. We cannot acknowledge historical dates of significance to people of color as moments of freedom while simultaneously condemning the system that made them possible. Those particular moments of positive progress for people of color can only be celebrated alongside the system that made it possible, as imperfect as it may be.

While many Christians have committed egregious sins against their fellow man, it was also those within Christianity that pointed out their hypocrisy and led to the change. No system is perfect, while men permeate and execute that system; however, the best systems of belief and doctrine refine themselves, as those within it learn and effect change by more accurately understanding its teachings. While created by God, Christianity is executed by man until He returns, and that allows errors and mistakes to occur even within the perfectly created system. Conversely, America and its system were created by men who tried to love God to the best of their ability, though erring often. Nevertheless, the principles embedded in America and its founding doctrines, rooted in perfect Scripture and the Christian system, are created by those same fallible men.

So, when modern warriors of perceived social justice tell us that America "has yet to live up to its promise," we should remember that the promise America is to live up to is a system that has made those people now free to say so. The principles of faithfulness to God, family, the sexes as created, children under the care of their parents, Church fealty, and hard work to achieve goals and leave a legacy behind are biblical principles worthy of our pursuit. Just as Onesimus was made Christian and assimilated into the Church, so too must those who feel wronged move forward and assimilate into the system that made them free. As they do, the system inherently becomes better, recognizing its past wrong and developing an understanding of itself.

Conclusion

There is no easy way to move forward. Many will consider this to be the slant of someone on the inside with no real experience of the situation. However, this is not true. Moreover, We cannot continue to condemn a system that had the parameters of freedom built into it, despite being misused at times to hurt others. We must see the difference between an error in the system and an error in the executors of the system.

Most of all, as scholars, theologians, public philosophers, or Christians, we cannot allow advantage to be taken upon the silence of Onesimus. Finally, the goal of this paper was to give you insight into what we must do to move forward or, conversely, why others refuse to move forward. These are the fundamental difference in the world views of those who reject moving forward or seeing that progress is within reach in earnest. Those in disagreement would, in many cases, see a *new system* in place. And that is the danger that lies ahead for us.

Our work is to engage the culture around us with reason and the Spirit of truth and hope, alongside Paul, that men will have a spirit to respond to our obsecration and do even more than we are asking (v. 21), and that through it, the God of all gods will restore our land and heal our nation to His own glory.

Divine Law and The Social Contract

Wyatt T. McIntyre

Introduction

The current debate, as it stands, is one which asks the fundamental question of compliance within a lawfully formed, orderly society. This question, simply put, is to what extent must the individual follow the authority of the state? Is the individual obligated to comply with the demands of a society in all ways because he or she has partaken in, and enjoyed the benefits of it?

Society exists through a social contract. Recognizing the mutual benefit of living in community with one another in a hierarchy governed by laws, institutions and traditions, individuals have agreed to trade certain natural rights, submitting to the authority of the state. This agreement does not need to be arrived at through explicit consent. Rather, it can be derived from the basic principle of *qui tacet consentire videtur*. Yet, if one consents to the exchange of natural rights for the blessing of society, natural liberty ceases to be the appeal in which the individual can utilize to deviate from the social contract. The only recourse against the social contract exists by the appeal to divine law.

The Social Contract

The social contract that exists within a society reflects a moral and an ethical obligation to the individual. This obligation stems from the realization that the individuals partake of the blessings of that society. As Socrates would argue in Plato's *Crito*, it is the agreement that the individual reaches with the state that allows for their birth, education, and physical training.¹ By ensuring the safety and security of the individual, apart from the state of nature, the society upholds its commitment to the individual.

The manner in which it fulfills its responsibility may not reflect a perfect adherence to fairness, justice or equality. Yet, it does represent a notable improvement in opportunity and survival than a pure and natural state of nature which does not offer the same benefits or protections that society will offer. Hospitals and medicine, schools and education, police and security, to name a few benefits, are the manner in which the state upholds its obligations under the social contract.

The individual is then bound to the laws, and the state which creates and enforces these laws, through a reciprocal agreement which is made when the individual partakes of the benefits of the society. In doing so he is now obligated to live a peaceable life within it, living justly within its framework and structure. This agreement begins at the youngest of ages through the system which allows for the birth of the individual. After all, as St. Thomas Aquinas would argue, "Those who are not present when a law is promulgated are bound to observe the law, insofar as it is notified or can be notified to them by others, after it has been promulgated."²

This reality is what prevents the individual from forsaking the social contract in order to revert to the state of nature, and thereby placing him or herself under the sole jurisdiction of natural liberty. The state of nature, as it has been conceived by social contract theorists, no longer exists for humanity. The implication of Socrates dialogue with Crito is that the social contract is generational, with the individual benefiting from it even prior to their birth.³ They

---

1   Plato. (1914). *Euthyphro, Apology, Crito, Phaedo, Phaedrus: English Text.* (H. N. Fowler, Trans.) (p. 177) (50d). Cambridge, MA; London, England: Harvard University Press.

2   St. Thomas Aquinas (2021). *Summa Theologiae: Prima Secundae*, 71-114. (Fr. Laurence Shapcote, OP, Trans.) (p. 202) (90 Art. 4). Green Bay, WI: Aquinas Institute, Inc.

3   Plato, 177 (50e).

may, by their consent, or the consent of the state, be transferred to another established social contract, but, in present reality, the individual may never be outside of the prevue of a social contract.

The Great Social Bargain

The scope and the framework of the social contract is dictated by the laws of a society. It is through these laws that the natural liberty of the individual is restrained. After all, "What man loses because of the social contract is his natural liberty and an unlimited limited right to anything that tempts him and that he can attain."[4] What this recognizes is that a society is formed when individuals come together through a common agreement that they will surrender certain freedoms and liberties in order to live together in peace and harmony. The unbridled will of the individual is then circumvented, as they recognize that they are no longer able to do as they place when they please without facing very specific consequences for their actions.

This does not mean though that the relationship is an entirely one-sided relationship. It does not mean that the individual does not gain anything in return. They are not simply required to give up their natural liberties in order to live within a society. As Jean-Jacques Rousseau would continue to state, "what he gains is civil liberty and property in all that he possesses."[5] There is a trade which occurs. Natural liberty may be given up, but civil liberty is obtained.

This great social bargain which then occurs, Rousseau argues, is one that represents a benefit to the individual. By living in a state of nature, governed by natural liberty, the individual becomes a servant to their base nature as they feed the impulse of appetite. Civil liberty, which is the product of society, represents moral freedom.

---

4   Jean-Jacques Rousseau. (2002) *The Social Contract and The First and Second Discourses.* (Susan Dunn, ed.) (p. 167) New Haven, CT; London, England: Yale University Press.
5   Ibid., 167.

Abiding in the laws of a legitimate society, the individual finds true liberty.[6]

This then creates a question. How far does this great social bargain extend? Is the individual always bound to comply with the laws of a society within the bounds of the social contract? Are there limits? If there are limits, what is the appeal which the individual can make in order to break the social contract?

The Appeal

The appeal is not one to natural liberty by virtue of the great social bargain. As the state of nature was abandoned, so too was the appeal to natural liberty. By engaging in the social contract, as it stands, the individual has stated that their own individual interests have an inherent value or place, but when they come in direct conflict with the interest of the society, or the interest of the whole they must acquiesce. The is the point of Socrates in *Crito* as he prepares himself for the death sentence handed to him by the state.

Even in the furthest reaches of a society that seeks to abandon hierarchy and structure, this has to be generally accepted. Even if one rejects Rousseau's notion of popular sovereignty for a system which takes on a different form that, the collectivist nature which a society takes on makes this the necessary reality. One must find a way in which they are able to align the individual good with that of the societal good.

This is not simply because they have, by partaking in the benefits of the society, agreed to abide by the terms of it, as Socrates argued. Rather, it is because the individual does not live in a state of nature. The terms and the condition of the social contract were such that natural liberty was exchanged for civil liberty. This was not based on a specific law or set of laws within a society. Rather, it was on the condition that society represented a benefit, offering protection, commerce, education, and other such blessings which could not be obtained within the state of nature.

---

6   Ibid., 167.

Likewise, to appeal to natural liberty is to appeal to a subjective view of how one's natural liberties are violated. Within the framework of a society, what one views to be a violation of this liberty may not be what another considers to be a violation. Thresholds for violations may be higher or lower based on the individual and the reason. For one then to claim that they need not abide by the social contract because of natural liberty represents an appeal that the individual has forfeited by living in the social contract.

As the individual is then unable to return to a state of nature, the appeal itself is one that is disingenuous. It is the individual wishing to partake in the blessings of a society, in the blessings of a social contract without having to live according to the terms of it.

Divine Law

To this end, if a social contract represents the highest law established by a society, the fundamental backbone by which the society itself is founded upon, it would seem there would be no appeal that the individual would have in objecting to the laws and the statutes of a society except within the framework which is established by that society. Thus, the individual would have a basic obligation to maintain and uphold the laws of that social contract above anything else, even when it is contrary to their deepest held beliefs or their freedoms.

Yet, whereas the social contract represents the highest law established by a society, a covenant that binds individuals together in a larger whole, it does not, in fact, represent the highest law. Existing outside the bounds of the social contract, governing its existence, and the existence of all laws, institutions, hierarchies and traditions established by humanity, is divine law. It is this divine law, established through the divine authority of humanity's Creator, that then represents the only counterforce to the social contract, representing the only real appeal that one has to the unjust acts which can be perpetrated through a society.

This is witnessed through the realization that, "… the force of law depends on the extent of its justice."[7] To this extent, "*non videteur esse lex, quae iusta non fuerit.*"[8] That is, namely, a law which, at its heart, is unjust does not actually appear to be a law at all.

The inherent problem that is arrived at is how does one know? As previously established laws within natural liberty, and the social contract are, to some level and extent, based on a subjective notion. Justice, as such, can be defined in a similar way, based on that which is deemed just by those who pass the laws. Thus, there must be an objective measure by which justice is ultimate recognized and gauged against. This is recognized by the fact that laws created by societies, created by men, can either be just, or unjust. If it is just, it binds the conscience to eternal law. If it is unjust, it is not, in fact, a law, and need not be followed.[9]

Whether a law is just, or unjust then requires a Divine Lawgiver who determines the definition and the nature of ethics, morality and justice. This Lawgiver must exist outside of the framework of human law in order to govern over it. It is only in doing so that He may, as such, not be swayed by the society itself, offering then an objective understanding rather than a subjective view. This then provides the framework by which all else may be judged and gives to the individual the ability to appeal what they might consider to be an unjust law or structure if a valid case can be made according to the statues of that Lawgiver.

It is, in fact, from this divine law that all other laws are derived. Without it there can be no eternal, natural or human laws. All law, by virtue of its very nature, stems from a transcending divine law from which all other laws flow. This is known by the fact that all just laws are arrived at through moral thought and ethical understanding. There can be no moral thought or ethical understanding within a divine law.

---

7   Aquinas, 239 (95, Art. 2).
8   Ibid., 239 (95, Art. 2).
9   Ibid. 249-250 (96, Art. 4).

DIVINE LAW AND THE SOCIAL CONTRACT 163

Even if one is to consider Natural Law to be the foundational law, one has to arrive at the conclusion that there is no provision for ethical behavior beyond the interest of the individual. This governs behavior even when gathered in a social framework, as is witnessed throughout nature. Thus laws, just laws must derive their authority from elsewhere, from something more, from something greater.

This is the foundation by which American society is founded. Governed by three formational documents declaring National (The Declaration of Independence), Political (The Constitution) and Individual (The Bill of Rights) freedom, it is the Declaration of Independence, which asserts the countries national sovereignty and freedom which forms the basis of its social contract, making society possible. This social contract, which recognizes the basis of natural liberty, yields to divine law, stating that it is only through divine law that a political and social bonds are strengthened or dissolved. To this end, though the instrument of Political and Individual freedom may not reference God or divine law, they do not need to. It is implied through the first document.

So it too is with all societies. Their social contract is made possible by divine law, and the divine lawgiver which determines the morality and the validity of laws themselves. It is that divine law which then governs over the individual with the social law serving as a placeholder for it insofar as it can be attested that these said laws affirm the dignity, respect, and sense of justice which is endowed upon the individual by their Creator. The moment that they cease to do so the law becomes null and void by this higher authority, potentially placing the social contract at risk.

Conclusion

Society exists through a social contract. This social contract provides for the individual a structure and framework by which they are able to live their lives apart from the base state of nature. This offers to them certain blessings as they are given the opportunity to flourish as they partake in what it has to offer for their benefit and their growth.

Yet, though this social contract provides for the individual and the community in a manner that it could not on its own, this does not mean that the social contract represents the highest law, nor does it mean that there is no recourse when a social contract acts in an unjust manner. When this occurs there is a higher authority in which an individual or a community may and must appeal to. This is the source from which all justice, morality and ethics flow. Establishing divine laws, this Divine Lawgiver offers recourse that supersedes the authority of the social contract. Thus, when the social contract provides for injustice, the only recourse left for the individual is to return to the divine law, which laws the foundation for all other law.

The Life of Abraham Lincoln

Arturo Gastelum

The life of Abraham Lincoln (1809-1865) has been subject to countless biographies, arguably more than any other American president. His life has been extensively scrutinized from manifold perspectives, yet his religious thought has been one of the least researched areas--and one of the most difficult to pinpoint accurately. In Lincoln, one encounters an enigmatic individual who, although he remained a public figure for an extensive period of his life, maintained privacy regarding his inner world. He masterfully managed to be both approachable and genuine. His mastery in storytelling and jokes won the admiration and sympathy of those who surrounded him, whether in his childhood, business, law, or politics. Yet it is believed that these gifts of oratory, humor, and humility were in large measure effectively used by Lincoln to keep his actual theological and philosophical beliefs private from others. In addition to Lincoln's discretion, other difficulties arise regarding biographers' biases towards Lincoln, as well as their own understanding of religion and philosophy. Christian biographers depict him as a Christian, skeptics as a skeptic, and deists as a deist. There is also the added complication of making sense of Lincoln's evolution of thought. In spite of the limitations, certain beliefs have been identified as being Lincoln's own.

The life of Lincoln has commonly been divided into four different periods, the first consisting of his boyhood, which culminated with the move from Indiana to Illinois (1809-1830). This portion of his life provided the foundation for the theological beliefs that Lincoln becomes more conscious of, and consistent in, throughout his life. His primary theological belief was a form of hard deterministic Calvinism. He believed in double-predestination, where God is the cause of all that comes to pass, including human agency.

This view supports the idea that both the means and the ends are predestined by God apart from the free will of individuals-- God is the sole agent of causation. This belief plays a central role in understanding Lincoln's moral compass and political wisdom. The second period covers his early manhood (1830-1837), when he left his father's household to reside in Springfield. This period served to cement his political and economic views regarding the benefits of the market economy, social mobility, the freedom of improvement through diligent work, and the ambition to pursue a life apart from the agrarian upbringing he had received in the Jeffersonian yeoman tradition, where rural self-sufficiency was the ideal. During the third period (1837-1861) Lincoln became a lawyer and pursued public office. During this period, Lincoln was exposed to ideas of the secular Enlightenment and its European thinkers. These thinkers promoted the notion of the sufficiency of rationalism--belief of the existence of self-evident truths, such as those found in Descartes' Cogito or as declared in the Declaration of Independence. These thinkers also supported empiricism--the idea that all knowledge is attained through the senses--through means of scientific inquiry to attain answers to metaphysical questions. The final period sees Lincoln as president (1861-1865). This period provided him with the most pointed theological, political, and moral challenges of his age. The questions Lincoln faced included the nature of the Union, the legitimacy of the doctrine of secession, popular sovereignty, nullification, slavery, emancipation, and the treatment of Southerners after defeat. All these questions tested the most prominent intellectuals of this time, yet none provided more intelligible, compelling, and clear answers to those problems than Lincoln. These challenges required responses that Lincoln formulated through reliance on his religious understanding. His religious beliefs served as the intellectual foundation to meet the challenges. Lincoln's responses are well known and documented through historical sources, most in his own superb penmanship, which remains unmatched by any other American President.

Abraham Lincoln held to a few doctrinal beliefs that were constant throughout his life. The most persistent and formative was the Doctrine of Necessity. This doctrine supports the idea that humans are void of free will and therefore have no moral responsibility for their actions. According to this view, human behavior is guided by inherent motives that determine human actions. These motives originate in a divine decree working in conjunction with all the particulars of an individual's historical context. The Doctrine of Necessity promotes a fatalistic conception of Providence—one where the end is predestined irrespective of an individual's actions, hence the idea of fate or fatalism. Yet, contrary to the common conception that holding to fatalism may lead a person to inaction, Lincoln's fatalistic view actually compelled him to action, fulfilling a grand purpose that had been appointed for him. It is a well-attested fact that Lincoln believed that the sovereign hand of God was at play in his life and that he himself was an instrument in God's predetermined plan. Lincoln used fatalism to reaffirm his commitment and to persevere in the causes that he believed were justified by a God who is both just and merciful.

The Doctrine of Necessity aided in developing Lincoln's magnanimous spirit. His greatness of soul resulted from his belief that whatever the actions people took, they simply could not do otherwise, all things considered. Lincoln did not hold people responsible for their actions because they were acting out of their historical situatedness. In other words, their actions were determined by their environment and their particular time and place in history, and they were simply carrying out a purpose they could not avoid. Throughout and after the war, Lincoln acted without malice towards Southerners. He believed they were living out the traditions, customs, and inculcated values cultivated over generations. They found themselves in their context and were merely acting out their part.

The patience that so characterized Lincoln was likewise connected with the Doctrine of Necessity. Time, change, and circumstances were needed for transformation to occur. He mastered the art of teleology (being goal oriented), working conscientiously to make gradual progress which, in the end, accomplished his purpose of informing the people's conscience and ultimately building consensus. Change was only possible once the circumstances had been altered to allow it, hence his characteristic patience, benign demeanor, compassionate heart, and steadfast determination to attain the predestined end.

The Doctrine of Necessity was impressed in his mind from early childhood as he was exposed to hard-predestinarian Baptist doctrine and worship. Lincoln grew up attending church and matured among a culture largely dominated by Christianity. The larger historical context in which Lincoln lived had a dominant influence in his life. However, the fact that the church was so divided along the lines of doctrine became a hindrance to Lincoln's own church attendance. The plurality of positions in religious dogmas, and the extensive, long-standing disputes amongst religious denominations became for him a compelling reason not to become a member of a specific church. How is one to choose among so many denominations and theological positions? That question remained unresolved throughout his life.

Theologically speaking, the church was not able to overcome the disputes regarding political matters, specifically slavery. The peculiar question of slavery became an obvious case where the church was unable to undo the theological gridlock arrived at by its key assumptions. The three main beliefs held by churches in the North and the South consisted of common sense realism, Republican principles, and a literal reading of the Bible. Common sense realism kept both sides entrenched in their own existing views. For the Southerner, having been brought up with the institution of slavery, it seemed perfectly natural that it should be continued and expanded. The moral sensitivities of the Southerners raised no objections to slavery's legitimacy and propriety. Northerners, on the other hand, grew up in the opposite context and arrived at the opposite conclusion. How could one determine which view was right? Common sense realism was unable to answer this question.

Both sides appealed to Republican principles of self-government—one to reinforce federalist views and the other to reinforce anti-federalism or the primacy of states' rights over and against the Union. Both appealed to the same history and documents, yet both arrived at opposite conclusions. Lastly, literalism likewise failed. The pressures of liberal theology compelled the Protestant church to highlight the importance of the plain meaning of the Bible. According to mainstream evangelicals, the Bible has a simple literal meaning that should be accessible to the uneducated without appeal to theological nuances and expertise. Yet, both sides found passages to justify their own views. The Old Testament and the New Testament both contain pro-slavery passages and anti-slavery passages. Each side appealed to their own selections for justification. Because of this inability to overcome differences, what was a theological issue regarding human equality and the dignity of the human person, became a political issue that required a political and therefore ultimately a military response. Lincoln lived through these disputes, and he brought his own theological understanding to bear in this context.

Lincoln's religious views evolved while in the presidency. When he came to the office, he was not an abolitionist. His first inaugural address was an exercise in temperance and restraint. It was the unfolding of the war that compelled Lincoln to meditate more deeply about God's providence, his moral attributes, and its implications for the war. His expectation at the beginning of the war was that the Lord would make his will clearly known by granting victory to the righteous side. Yet the war dragged on. This made it clear that God was acting in mysterious ways, that neither side was on the side of truth entirely, and that the issue of slavery—a mutually committed sin—was the cause of the war. God in his providence had allowed it to remain, yet He was now pleased to remove it. Both sides suffered for their sin of slavery, both were complicit in its origin and development, therefore both were afflicted. Lincoln made use of his Doctrine of Necessity to pierce into the inscrutable divine will. His last theological remarks remain permanently and publicly declared in his second inaugural address, where Lincoln affirmed his belief in God—his lordship over all things, the inscrutability of his will, the immortality of the soul with full awareness in the afterlife, and the wisdom of the Bible for morality. Lincoln held steadfastly the belief in the need for forgiveness towards the sin of others. Yet Lincoln stopped short of professing belief in Christ and the need for redemption. Those who impute Christian faith to Lincoln do so in light of his moral uprightness, and not in light of an outward profession of belief in Christ. Lincoln can be best described as a deist who assigned God the traditional moral attributes of goodness, justice, mercy, holiness, and truth. His views on religion reflect the legacy of the Enlightenment rationalism regarding Christian doctrine. Lincoln exercised a well-noted interest in the moral complexities of the human mind in regard to human behavior to oneself and one-another, yet Lincoln made little of the more fundamental question regarding the relationship and responsibility of mankind to God. It is not clear that Lincoln understood the sin of mankind as rooted in our failure to know and acknowledge God as the creator, ruler, and redeemer. Lincoln did not note how mankind's unbelief was without excuse for failing to see the clarity of God's existence from the created order as described by the Apostle Paul in Romans 1:18-20. Lincoln's merits for his erudite performance as a president and leader of this nation have been extensively documented. Yet the question remains regarding Lincoln's lack of engagement regarding the ethics of belief. Are humans morally responsible to know and acknowledge God? Or is the existence of God beyond the capabilities of the human mind to address? The doctrine of necessity provided Lincoln with the rationale to excuse human beings for not seeing what is clear about God, yet it is not clear that one is rationally justified in adopting a view of a deterministic God without first addressing the epistemological questions that are used to arrive at that conclusion. Abraham Lincoln's herculean task to solve the practical challenges of divine mystery in regard to the Civil War stand as a testimony of how one can be consumed by the existential challenges about us without first addressing the epistemological bases from which those challenges ought to be addressed. Abraham Lincoln is both an inspiration and a warning; a model of uprightness and genius that should give us pause to not overlook the more foundational assumptions in understanding human conflict. Can one be a great unifier of man-to-man while ignoring the need for unity between fallen humanity and God? Ethical unity presupposes and requires epistemic unity. Unity if it is to last must have a foundation rooted in the metaphysical realities of the world. May we learn of the unsurpassed positive example of Abraham Lincoln as well as his negative example in neglecting epistemic questions regarding the ethics of belief.

Bibliography:

Guelzo, C. Allen. 2005. Abraham Lincoln: Redeemer President. Grand Rapids: William B. Eerdmans Publishing Company.

Barton, E. William. 2005. The Soul of Abraham Lincoln. New York: University of Illinois.

Wilson, L. Douglas. 1998. Honor's Voice: The Transformation of Abraham Lincoln. New York: Vintage Books.

Noll, A. Mark. 2002. America's God: From Jonathan Edwards to Abraham Lincoln. New York: Oxford University Press.

Book Review
Crisp, Oliver. Jonathan Edwards Among the Theologians. Grand Rapids: Eerdmans Publishing, 2015.

Arturo Gastelum

Oliver Crisp provides an exposition of the central tenets of Jonathan Edwards's theology to illustrate how a great mind engages with the most pressing contemporary issues—given its historical context—while employing new theological and philosophical methodologies with the aim of providing sound doctrine with a firmer footing. The tension that arises between upholding the historically accepted orthodox Christian Catholic beliefs while defending them through the use of new epistemological approaches, serves as a study in exploring the limits of the compatibility of the two. It is here that Jonathan Edwards' suits the demands of such an inquiry. He lived within a century of the highest achievements of Reformed theology and right in the middle of the rationalist Enlightenment of the eighteenth-century. How far can a great thinker go in answering the inquiries of skeptics without compromising his/her standing with orthodoxy? And what beliefs count as primary to qualify a thinker as belonging within the established tradition? Furthermore, what implications should be derived from the example of Jonathan Edwards for contemporary theologians and philosophers since we are now faced with the compounded challenges of both modernity and postmodernity? An answer to these questions is attempted through a comparative analysis of Edwards' main theological positions juxtaposed with those held by prominent theologians, who varied in their orthodox status.

The doctrines selected for examination in this work were some of the most widely contested beliefs in the Enlightenment. They constitute central tenets of orthodoxy established in the ecumenical creeds and councils (e.g., Nicea, Chalcedon, Orange, etc.) and were further developed in the Reformation (i.e., Dordt, Heidelberg, Belgic, Thirty-Nine Articles, and the Westminster Confession). Jonathan Edwards came into the discourse after these doctrines were formulated; yet having lived after their formulation, he ventured to defend and, in some cases, reinterpret those existing doctrines. His most notable deviations are singled out by Oliver Crisp to raise awareness of their problematic implications and to call the reader to think further about the boundaries of orthodoxy.

The general layout of the book contains nine chapters. The first chapter introduces the reader to the relationship that Jonathan Edwards held with his contemporary Reformed thinkers. This chapter explains the commonly held beliefs by the Reformers and it shows how Jonathan Edwards did not follow in the tradition of confessional theologians (e.g., Francis Turretin, Charles Hodge, and B. B. Warfield). Edwards is considered by Oliver Crisp as a great thinker whose contribution lies in seeing the importance of issues clearly, seeking to elevate the discussion to a new level of clarity and sophistication, even though this may come at the cost of being mistaken in some instances.[1] The second chapter addresses the nature of God, specifically his aseity and simplicity as understood historically through Anselm. Here a contrast is provided between the standard metaphysical conception of God over and against Edwards' radical departures by holding to panentheism, emanation, idealism, and the denial of secondary causes in momentarianism. These doctrinal departures are the main unorthodox views that Edwards held. Then, in chapter three, Edwards' view of the Trinity is explained. Edwards' views are presented mostly in accord with orthodoxy. The excellence of the internal coherence of the ontological, ethical, and economic aspects of the Trinity are elucidated. In chapter four a

---

1   Oliver Crisp, *Jonathan Edwards among the Theologians* (Grand Rapids: Eerdmans Publishing, 2015), xviii.

new element is pointedly brought up. In comparing Jacob Arminius' view on creation with Edwards', it becomes clear that Arminius holds to the traditional view, yet Edwards radically ventures into panentheism. Then the question is raised regarding the common judgement placed upon the orthodoxy of Arminius versus the highly exalted position of Edwards in the Reformed tradition. The question arises: how is one excluded from Reformed theology while the other is praised? Arminius is excluded on the grounds of soteriology and middle knowledge, but Edwards remains praised in spite of his panentheism, idealism, and momentarianism? This contentious question compels the reader to analyze the basis upon which Orthodoxy is predicated. Are some beliefs more important than others? If so, how does one decide? This question persists throughout the book. The reader is compelled through similar theological juxtapositions to provide a rationale for that and other apparent discrepancies in expectation and theological standards. In chapter five, the compatibilist and libertarian conceptions of free agency are discussed within the larger context of the sovereignty of God and moral responsibility. Jonathan Edwards positive contribution to this subject is acknowledged. In the last three chapters, the topics are centered upon: The doctrine of original sin in regard to double guilt (imputation and actual sin); the penal substitution view of atonement and its compatibility with Bellamy's view; and an overall reappraisal of the orthodoxy of Jonathan Edwards in light of the problematic doctrines explored in the preceding chapters.

The theme that runs throughout the work is the belief that "Edwards still has things to teach us today, in matters of theological method as well as doctrinal substance."[2] The method consists in Edward making use of the new philosophical tools made available by early Enlightenment philosophy to re-envision Reformed theology.[3] Crisp, through Edwards' example calls the contemporary theologian to do likewise in our current setting—appropriate the epistemological tools available to reinterpret Christian theol-

---

2   Crisp, p. xx.
3   Ibid., p. 4.

ogy and thus present it to our contemporaries in a new light. A noble call that carries with it the risks that Edwards' himself fell into when pursuing his approach; we run the risk of undermining already well-developed theological formulations that may suffer because of one's attempt to rework what was already there. In Edwards' case, unlike the case of Charles Hodge and other confessional theologians, Edwards introduces doctrines that undermined the work already attained by earlier theologians in the creeds and councils of the Reformation. The formulation provided in the Westminster Confession of Faith addressed the nature of the aseity and simplicity of God in chapter 2 along with the relation between primary and secondary causes regarding God's creation in chapter 3. Jonathan Edwards departed from the existing corpus of theological doctrine which was the product of much discussion undergone by the most insightful pastors and teachers of the church at the time, which continues to be the high watermark of the Reformation since it built upon the preceding creeds and councils. The theological errors pointed out by Crisp, were previously pointed out by Charles Hodge—as acknowledged by Crisp himself—as departures from the work already done.[4] Perhaps, prior to venturing in attempting to answer inquiries to the Christian faith, a lesson can be drawn from the example of Jonathan Edwards i.e., ensure that one is properly understanding and making use of the work already accomplished by believers in the history of the church—especially when it was the work accomplished through the process of much discussion—before venturing into new approaches. Perhaps the work or theological foundation has already been done and our epistemic responsibility is to build upon it and not to obscure or undermine what was already accomplished. The historic Christian faith may be perhaps better established and more profitably studied when learning from the creeds and councils, since they are the product of many minds engaged in formulating a theological doctrine which may provide a better thought out expression than the one attained by the individual thinker who while may be helpful

---

4   Ibid., p. 179-180.

in some areas, may bring grave errors in others, as in the case of Jonathan Edwards.

Advertisements

Logos College of Liberal Arts

You may now sign up to take core courses for the Liberal Arts degree at Logos College of Liberal Arts. Core courses are taken asynchronous online at your own pace. Sign up for Introduction to Philosophy, Logic, Introduction to Ethics, World Religions, and Introduction to Christianity. Coming soon: Philosophy of Religion, History of Philosophy, and Theological Foundation.

To register for classes:
https://logos-college-of-liberal-arts.teachable.com/

Public Philosophy Press

Public Philosophy Press has a growing catalog of books and e-books. New titles are coming summer of 2022.

To view our current catalog:
https://publicphilosophypress.com/

Wisdom Academies

Courses are now being offered on uncommon sense common sense wisdom at the Wisdom Academies.

Wisdom Academies is a Distance Education Provider under the auspices of Aquinas Leadership School, LLC. It furnishes self-paced, non-credit bearing college-level academic courses through self-study, video, email communication with educational consultants.

To register for classes:
https://www.wisdomacademies.com/p/welcome-to-wisdom-academies.html

www.ingramcontent.com/pod-product-compliance
Lightning Source LLC
Chambersburg PA
CBHW030300100526
44590CB00012B/455